HMH |  into **Reading**™

my **Book** ②

Authors and Advisors

Alma Flor Ada • Kylene Beers • F. Isabel Campoy
Joyce Armstrong Carroll • Nathan Clemens
Anne Cunningham • Martha C. Hougen
Elena Izquierdo • Carol Jago • Erik Palmer
Robert E. Probst • Shane Templeton • Julie Washington

Contributing Consultants

David Dockterman • Mindset Works®
Jill Eggleton

Printed in the U.S.A.

ISBN   978-0-544-45883-3

9 10   0868   27 26 25 24 23 22

4500845689   C D E F G

HMH

(into) Reading™

myBook **2**

MODULE 3

Meet in the Middle

🌐 **SOCIAL STUDIES CONNECTION:** Solving Problems............ 8

Meet Me Halfway... 12

INFORMATIONAL TEXT

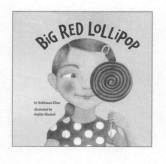

Big Red Lollipop.. 14

by Rukhsana Khan • illustrated by Sophie Blackall
REALISTIC FICTION

› On My Own
The Best Name... 36

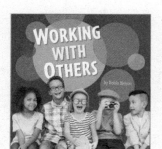

Working with Others..................... 40

by Robin Nelson
INFORMATIONAL TEXT

› On My Own
I Respectfully Disagree!.......................... 54

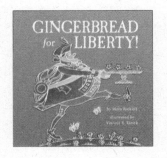

Gingerbread for Liberty! 58

by Mara Rockliff • illustrated by Vincent X. Kirsch

BIOGRAPHY

› On My Own
An American Hero 80

Pepita and the Bully 84

by Ofelia Dumas Lachtman • illustrated by Alex Pardo DeLange

REALISTIC FICTION

› On My Own
More Than One Way to Win 106

Be a Hero! Work It Out! 110

by Ruben Cooley

MEDIA: INFOGRAPHIC

Let's Wrap Up! 118

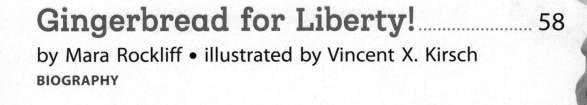

MODULE 4

Once Upon a Time

🌐 **SOCIAL STUDIES CONNECTION:** Storytelling................ 120

Recipe for a Fairy Tale.................... 124

RECIPE

How to Read a Story...................... 126

by Kate Messner • illustrated by Mark Siegel
PROCEDURAL TEXT

› On My Own
How to Find a Story 148

A Crow, a Lion, and a Mouse! Oh, My!...................... 152

retold by Crystal Hubbard
DRAMA

› On My Own
The Wind and the Sun........................... 162

6

Hollywood Chicken 166
by Lisa Fleming • illustrated by Will Terry
FANTASY

‣ On My Own
The Best View 184

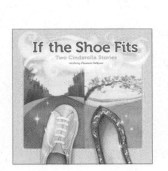

If the Shoe Fits: Two Cinderella Stories 188
retold by Pleasant DeSpain
FAIRY TALES

‣ On My Own
The Elves and the Shoemaker 202

Those Clever Crows 206
from *The New York Times*
MEDIA: VIDEO

Let's Wrap Up! 210

Glossary 212

Index of Titles and Authors 218

Meet in the Middle

"You must speak words that matter."

—Kate DiCamillo

? Essential Question

How can people work out disagreements?

Get Curious
Video

Words About Solving Problems

Complete the Vocabulary Network to show what you know about the words.

compromise

Meaning: A **compromise** is when people agree to something by each giving up a little of what they want.

Synonyms and Antonyms	Drawing

decision

Meaning: When you make a **decision**, you make up your mind about something.

Synonyms and Antonyms	Drawing

disagreement

Meaning: In a **disagreement**, people have different ideas about things.

Synonyms and Antonyms	Drawing

MEET ME HALFWAY

What does it mean when people say, "Let's meet in the middle"? They are talking about **compromise**, or a way to end a disagreement.

When people compromise, they each give up a little of what they want. These comic strips show examples of compromise.

13

Prepare to Read

GENRE STUDY **Realistic fiction** stories are made up but could happen in real life. As you read *Big Red Lollipop,* look for:

- characters who act and talk like real people
- a lesson the main character learns
- problems that real people might have

SET A PURPOSE As you read, stop and think if you don't understand something. Reread, ask yourself questions, use what you already know, and look for visual clues to help you understand the text.

POWER WORDS

invited

screams

plead

musical

shove

scoots

greedy

scurries

Meet Rukhsana Khan.

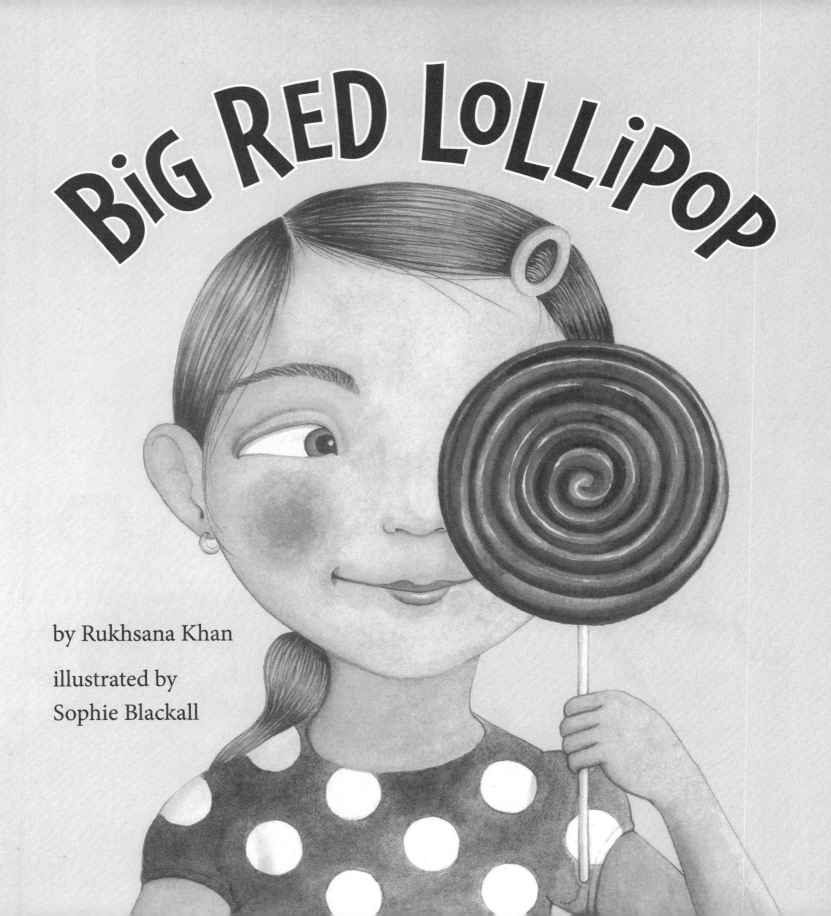

BiG RED LoLLiPoP

by Rukhsana Khan

illustrated by
Sophie Blackall

I'm so excited I run all the way home from school.

"Ami! I've been invited to a birthday party! There's going to be games and toys, cake and ice cream! Can I go?"

Sana screams, "I wanna go too!"

Ami says, "What's a birthday party?"

"It's when they celebrate the day they were born."

"Why do they do *that*?"

"They just do! Can I go?"

Sana screams, "I wanna go too!"

"I can't take *her*! She's not invited."

"Why not?" says Ami.

"They don't do that here!"

Ami says, "Well that's not fair. You call up your friend and ask if you can bring Sana, or else you can't go."

"But Ami! They'll laugh at me! They'll never invite me to another party again!"

Sana screams, "I wanna go too!"

17

I say, "Look, Sana, one day you'll get invited to your own friends' parties. Wouldn't you like that better?"

"No! I wanna go now!"

I beg and plead, but Ami won't listen. I have no choice. I have to call. Sally says, "All right." But it doesn't sound all right. I know she thinks I'm weird.

At the party, I'm the only one who brought her little sister. Sana has to win all the games, and when she falls down during musical chairs, she cries like a baby.

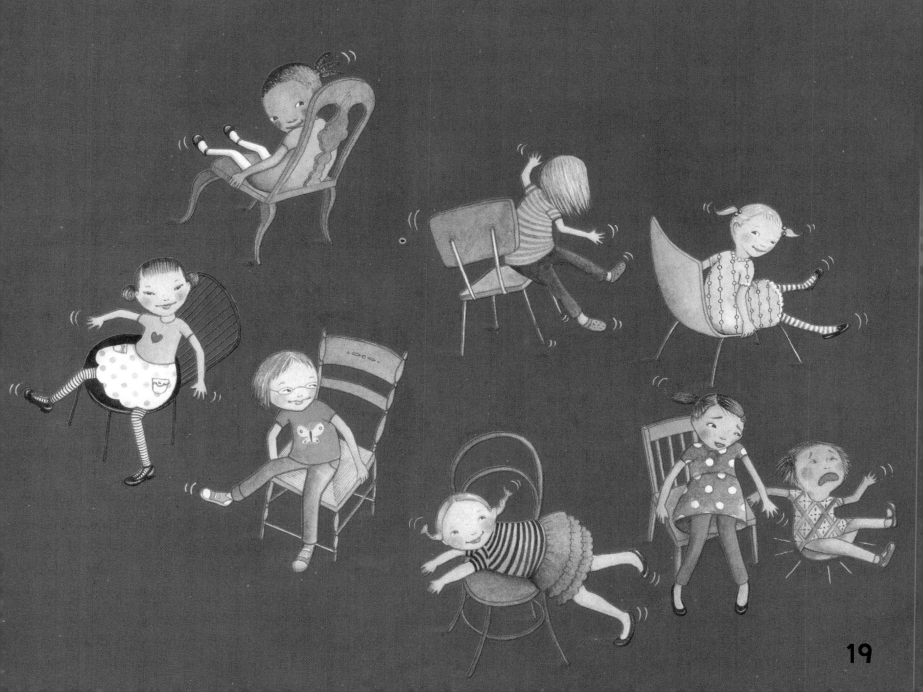

Before we leave the party, Sally's mom gives us little bags. Inside there are chocolates and candies, a whistle, a ruby ring, and a big red lollipop! Sana eats her big red lollipop on the way home in the car. I save mine for later.

Sana doesn't know how to make things last. By bedtime, her candies are all gone, her whistle is broken, and the ruby in her ring is missing. I put my big red lollipop on the top shelf of the fridge to have in the morning.

All night I dream about how good it will taste.

21

In the morning, I get up early to have it. Sana's already up. When she sees me, she runs away.

I open the fridge door. All that's left of my lollipop is a triangle stuck to a stick.

"SANA!"

I hear a sound in the front hall closet. I should have known. That's where she always hides.

I shove aside the coats and boots. "I'm going to *get* you!"

Quick as a rat, she scoots through my legs and runs around and around the living room, the dining room, the kitchen, yelling, "Ami! Ami! Help! Help!"

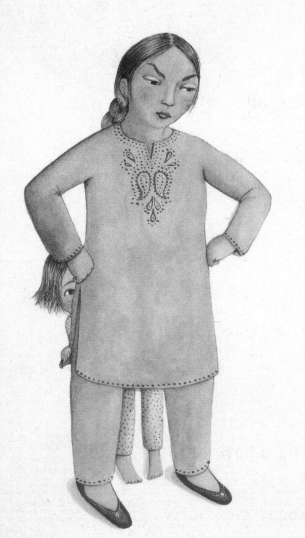

Ami comes out, rubbing her eyes. Sana runs behind Ami, where I can't get her.

"What's going on out here?" says Ami.

Sana says, "Rubina's trying to get me!"

Ami puts her hands on her hips. "Are you trying to get your little sister again?"

"She ate my *lollipop*! The greedy thing! She ate it!"

Ami says, "For shame! It's just a lollipop! Can't you *share* with your little sister?"

I want to cry, but I don't.

Sana runs to the fridge and brings back the triangle stuck to the stick. "Look! I didn't eat *all* of your lollipop! I left the triangle for you!"

"See?" says Ami. "She didn't eat *all* of it. She's sharing with you! Go ahead. Take the triangle."

So I have to take it.

"Go ahead. *Eat* the triangle."

But I don't. With all my might, I throw it across the room. It skitters under the sofa.

Sana scurries after it and eats that too.

The worst thing is that all the girls at school know if they invite me to their birthday parties, I have to bring Sana.

I don't get any invitations for a really long time.

Then one day Sana comes home waving an invitation.

"Ami! I've been invited to a birthday party! There's going to be games and toys and cake and ice cream! Can I go?"

Our little sister Maryam screams, "I wanna go too!"

Sana says, "No! I can't take *her*! She's not invited!"

Ami says, "Well . . . it's only fair. You went to Rubina's friend's party, now Rubina and Maryam can go to your friend's party." I say, "Leave me out of it."

Ami says, "Fine then, you have to take Maryam."

Now it's Sana's turn to beg and plead. Ami won't listen. Sana's begging so hard she's crying, but still Ami won't listen.

I *could* just watch her have to take Maryam. I *could* just let her make a fool of herself at that party. I *could* just let her not be invited to any more parties, but something makes me tap Ami on the shoulder.

"What?"

"Don't make Sana take Maryam to the party."

"No?" says Ami.

"No," I say.

Ami thinks for a moment, then says, "Okay."

So Sana gets to go by herself.

After the party, I hear a knock on my door.

"What do *you* want?" I ask Sana.

"Here." She hands me a big green lollipop. "This is for you."

"Thanks," I say.

After that we're friends.

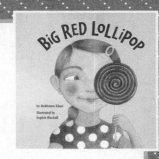

Use details from *Big Red Lollipop* to answer these questions with a partner.

1. **Monitor and Clarify** How did using what you know about birthday parties help you understand the events in the story?

2. How did the other girls at the party feel about Rubina bringing Sana? Use details from the text and pictures to explain your answer.

3. Why do you think Rubina tells Ami to let Sana go to the party without Maryam? What does that tell you about Rubina?

Listening Tip

Look at your partner as you listen. Wait until your partner finishes speaking before you talk.

Write a Journal Entry

PROMPT How would the story be different if Sana were telling it? Think about the story events as you explain your ideas.

PLAN First, choose one event in the story to write about. Fill in the chart with what Sana does, says, and feels during that event.

Actions	Words	Feelings

WRITE Now write a journal entry from Sana's point of view that describes the event. Remember to:

- Include details that show what Sana does, says, and feels.

- Use the words *I* and *me* to tell the story as Sana would.

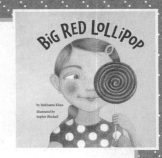

_____

_____

_____

_____

_____

_____

_____

_____

_____

_____

Prepare to Read

GENRE STUDY **Realistic fiction** stories are made up but could happen in real life.

MAKE A PREDICTION Preview "The Best Name." In this story, a family has a new pet dog. They also have a problem. What do you think it is?

_____

_____

_____

_____

_____

_____

SET A PURPOSE Read to find out how a family works together to solve a problem and to see if your prediction is correct. If not, use what you know about realistic fiction to make a new prediction.

The Best Name

READ As you read, ask yourself questions about parts that don't make sense. Then go back and reread those parts.

We just got a dog. He is so lovable! He has a very sweet face and a shiny red coat. The only problem is what to name him. Everyone in the family has an opinion. Dad wants Rolf because that is how the dog's bark sounds. Mom thinks he looks like an Ernie. My brother Sam wants to call him Digger. I want to let the dog pick, but I'm not sure how to do it.

> **Close Reading Tip**
> Underline the problem in the story.

CHECK MY UNDERSTANDING

How does the family feel about their dog? How can you tell?

_____

_____

_____

READ Who solves the problem? <u>Underline</u> the solution.

Close Reading Tip

Write **C** when you make a connection.

"Family meeting!" Mom announces when we sit at the table for dinner. "We're not going anywhere," she says, "until we all agree on a name for our dog."

Everyone argues for the name they like best.

"I know!" I say. "We can use all the names! We can use the *R* from Rolf, the *E* from Ernie, and the *D* from Digger!"

"*RED!*" everyone shouts together.

Red barks and wags his tail. We all laugh.

"Looks like we have a winner!" Dad says.

CHECK MY UNDERSTANDING

Who is the narrator? How does this point of view help you understand the story?

_____

_____

_____

_____

WRITE ABOUT IT How would the story be different if it were written from Red's point of view? Describe the events the way Red would. Include details about what he thinks, does, and feels.

_____

_____

_____

_____

_____

_____

_____

_____

_____

_____

_____

Prepare to Read

GENRE STUDY **Informational text** is nonfiction. It gives facts about a topic. As you read *Working with Others,* look for:

- the main topic and details
- headings that stand out
- photographs

SET A PURPOSE You know that informational texts include facts. Make a **prediction,** or good guess, about the information you will read about in this text. Read to see if your prediction is right. If not, make a new prediction.

POWER WORDS

blamed

argue

respectful

practice

Build Background: Teamwork and Cooperation

WORKING WITH OTHERS

by Robin Nelson

You work and play with other people every day. Most of the time, you get along well, but sometimes people do or say things that you don't like.

Maybe someone takes one of your toys or you are blamed for something you didn't do. Maybe someone calls you a mean name or you feel left out. Maybe you argue with a friend. These things can make you angry. It is okay to feel angry sometimes, and it is okay to have conflicts with people.

What do people do when conflicts make them angry? Some people yell and scream when they feel angry. Some people even hit other people. Yelling, screaming, and hitting do not solve conflicts. They hurt people and make problems worse. Some people walk away from conflicts. They want to be alone when they feel angry. They need time to calm down.

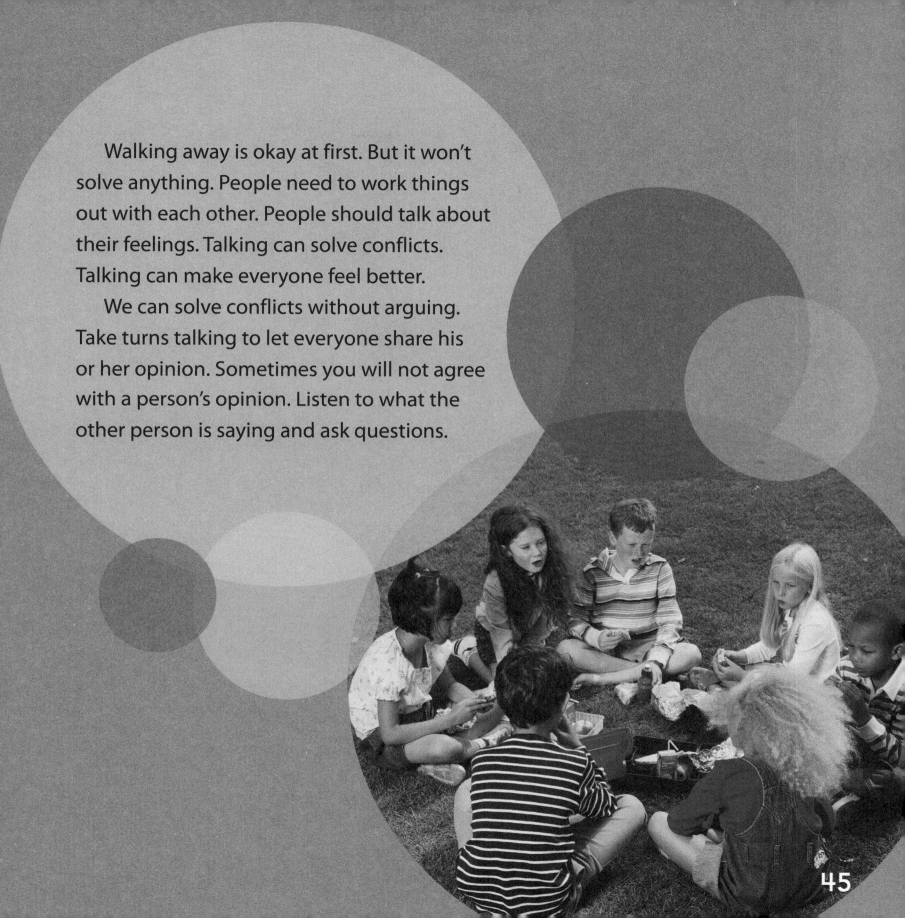

Walking away is okay at first. But it won't solve anything. People need to work things out with each other. People should talk about their feelings. Talking can solve conflicts. Talking can make everyone feel better.

We can solve conflicts without arguing. Take turns talking to let everyone share his or her opinion. Sometimes you will not agree with a person's opinion. Listen to what the other person is saying and ask questions.

Use respectful words. Don't call each other names. Apologize when you are wrong. Make sure everyone has a chance to speak. Then you can solve conflicts together. Think of ideas to solve the conflicts. Decide which ideas will work best.

If you are stuck, ask an adult to help you solve the conflicts. Ask someone to help who will listen and not take sides.

You might have to compromise. Compromise means both sides must give up something to solve conflicts.

Solving conflicts peacefully takes practice. Work together! Solve conflicts as a team. Talk them out, and everyone will be happy!

48

Dealing with Anger

What do you do when you feel angry? You might feel too angry to talk about how you feel. Here are some ways for you to calm down and get the anger out.

- Take deep breaths and count slowly.

- Write down what happened and how you feel about it.

- Draw a picture.

- Listen to calm music.

- Read a book.

- Take a walk or do some other kind of exercise.

- Pound on a pillow.

- Stomp your feet.

Talking Things Out

When you feel a little better, it is time to talk. Here are some things to remember when talking things out.

- Tell the other person how you feel and why you feel that way. Be honest. Ask that person how he or she feels.

- Remember that your body also tells a person how you are feeling. Show that you care about what he or she is saying. Don't cross your arms or make faces.

- Look at the person you are speaking to. Do the same thing when the other person is speaking to you.

- Listen carefully to what the other person has to say.

- Wait for your turn to speak.

- Apologize when you are wrong or if you hurt someone's feelings.

- Try to find a way to do things differently next time.

Use details from *Working with Others* to answer these questions with a partner.

1. **Make and Confirm Predictions** What predictions did you make about the facts you would read in this text? What were you right about? What was different?

2. Use information from the text to describe things that can cause a conflict.

3. Why is it a good idea to make sure that everyone has a chance to speak when solving conflicts?

Talking Tip

Ask to learn more about one of your partner's ideas. Complete the sentence below.

Please explain _____.

Write an Explanation

PROMPT How do you solve a conflict with someone? Use details from the words and photos to explain your answer.

PLAN First, make notes about steps you can follow when you are having a conflict.

WRITE Now write an explanation that tells someone what to do to solve a conflict. Remember to:

- Look for details in the text that are good examples of how to solve a conflict.

- Use action words that tell your reader exactly what to do.

_____

_____

_____

_____

_____

_____

_____

_____

_____

_____

Prepare to Read

GENRE STUDY **Informational text** is nonfiction. It gives facts about a topic.

MAKE A PREDICTION Preview "I Respectfully Disagree!" You know that informational text has facts and details about a topic. What do you think you'll learn from reading this text?

_____

_____

_____

_____

_____

_____

_____

SET A PURPOSE Read to find out how to respectfully disagree with someone.

I Respectfully Disagree!

READ What is the topic of this text?

Have you and a friend ever had different opinions about something? Of course you have! Everyone has an opinion. Sometimes a friend's opinion won't match yours. It is important to be respectful when this happens. Remember to be polite and caring. Just because he or she has a different opinion doesn't mean you can't still be friends!

Close Reading Tip

Circle words you don't know. Then figure them out. If you need to, look them up in a dictionary.

CHECK MY UNDERSTANDING

What is the text mainly about?

_____

_____

_____

READ <u>Underline</u> the sentence that tells the central idea on this page. Which details tell more about the central idea?

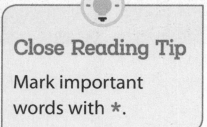

Close Reading Tip

Mark important words with *.

It can be hard to understand why a friend doesn't share your opinion. However, don't call your friend names or say your friend is wrong. Just because a person has a different opinion doesn't mean it's wrong. Say "I respectfully disagree" and explain why. Sometimes, no matter what you say, you and your friend will not agree. It might be that the one thing you do agree on is that you disagree! In this case you can say, "Let's agree to disagree!"

CHECK MY UNDERSTANDING

Look back at the prediction you made on page 54. Was it correct? Why or why not?

_____

_____

_____

_____

_____

Cite Text Evidence

WRITE ABOUT IT Do you think knowing how to disagree respectfully is important? Why or why not? Use details from the text to explain your opinion.

Prepare to Read

GENRE STUDY **Biographies** tell about real people's lives. As you read *Gingerbread for Liberty!,* look for:

- information about why this person is important
- the place where the person lived, worked, or traveled
- ways the person has made a difference

SET A PURPOSE Read to find out the most important ideas in each part. Then **synthesize,** or put together these ideas in your mind, to find out what the text really means to you.

POWER WORDS

booming

skill

threatening

persuade

Meet Mara Rockliff.

GINGERBREAD for LIBERTY!

by Mara Rockliff

illustrated by
Vincent X. Kirsch

Everyone in Philadelphia knew the gingerbread baker.
His honest face . . . his booming laugh . . .

And, of course, his gingerbread—the best in all the thirteen colonies. His big, floury hands turned out castles and queens, horses and cows and hens—each detail drawn in sweet, buttery icing with the greatest skill and care.

And yet, despite his care, there always seemed to be some broken pieces for the hungry children who followed their noses to the spicy-smelling shop.

"No empty bellies here!" the baker bellowed. "Not in *my* America!"

For once upon a time, he had been young and hungry too. And he had followed his own nose to this New World, where a hard-working young man could open his own bakery and always have enough to eat.

But now, something was in the air (besides the smell
of baking gingerbread).
Newspapers shouted

REVOLUTION! INDEPENDENCE! LIBERTY!

Boys rolled up blankets, shouldered guns, and kissed mothers
goodbye.

The baker hung his apron up. He dusted flour off his hands.

"Where are you going?" asked his wife.

"To fight for my America!" he said. "I was a soldier once."

"That was long ago and far away," she said. "You are a baker now,
and you are old and fat."

The baker knew his wife was right.
But he knew also that he loved his country.
Somehow, he had to find a way to help.

He packed his bags and went to join General Washington.

General Washington did not say the baker was
old and fat. General Washington was too polite.
Anyway, he had other troubles on his mind.

The baker rolled up his sleeves.
"No empty bellies here," he told General Washington.
"Not in *my* America!"
But bigger trouble was on the way.

Across the ocean. . .

The king of England wrote to other rulers and hired THEIR armies to help him squash the revolution.

When the ships sailed into sight, even General Washington turned pale. Who had ever seen such an army?

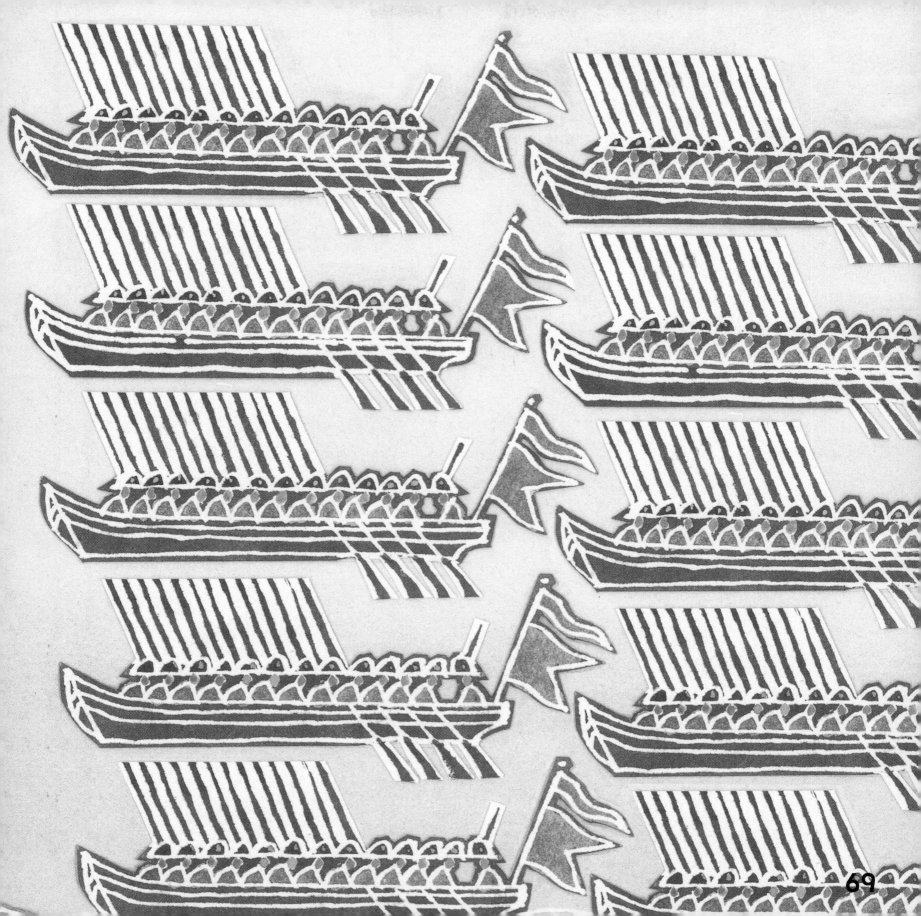

"These soldiers come from the land where I was born,"
the baker told General Washington. "Let me go speak to them.
Perhaps I can **persuade** them we are not their enemies.
Perhaps I can even persuade them to switch sides!"

"If you are caught, you will be killed," Washington warned.
The baker smiled. "Then I must not be caught."

In the darkest hour of the night, he rowed across the bay. With each dip of his oars, he thought of words to win the soldiers over to the American cause.

REVOLUTION! (splash)
Befreiung!

INDEPENDENCE! (splash)
Unabhängigkeit!

LIBERTY! (splash, splash)
Freiheit!

71

But when he looked into their hungry faces, all his fine
words slipped away.

What could he say?

"I have a bakeshop . . ." he began.

As the baker spoke, the soldiers seemed to see the fragrant
steam rising from his ovens. They could almost smell the spicy
gingerbread, and taste the sweet, buttery icing on their tongues.

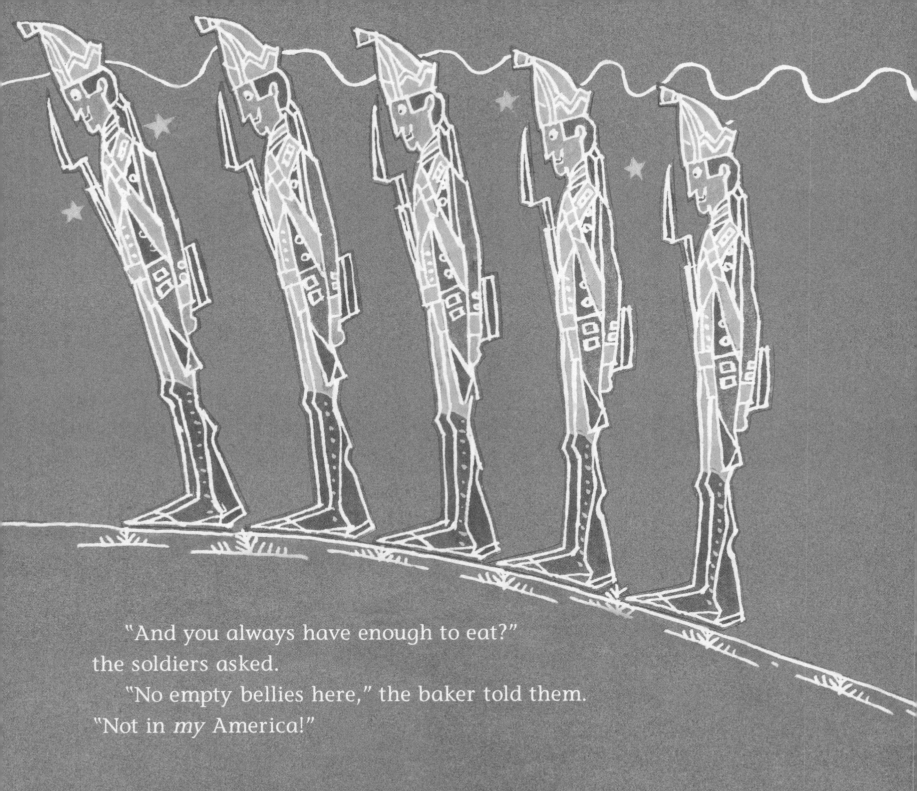

"And you always have enough to eat?"
the soldiers asked.

"No empty bellies here," the baker told them.
"Not in *my* America!"

Across the ocean. . .

Many, many loaves—and battles!—later . . .

THE BRITISH HAVE SURRENDERED!
THE REVOLUTION IS OVER!
WE WON!

"My work is done!" the baker cried.

Washington said, "Not quite."

Did he bake the British soldiers gingerbread for their dessert?

We'll never know . . .

They didn't leave a crumb.

Use details from *Gingerbread for Liberty!* to answer these questions with a partner.

1. **Synthesize** Why did the baker want to join General Washington? How did that decision change history?

2. What does the author want to describe? What does the illustrator want to show?

3. How did General Washington's feelings about the baker change? What do you think Washington learned from this experience?

Listening Tip

Look at your partner as you listen. Nod your head to show you are interested.

Write a Conversation

PROMPT How do you think General Washington reacted when the baker explained what happened with the hired soldiers? Use details from the text and pictures to explain your ideas.

PLAN First, draw a picture of the baker talking to General Washington. Show how each character feels. Add speech balloons to show what they are saying.

WRITE Now write a conversation between the baker and General Washington. Have the baker explain how he talked the hired soldiers out of fighting. Remember to:

- Look for details in the text that give clues about how General Washington might react.

- Include feeling words such as *amazed, proud, scared,* and *thrilled* to help the characters express how they feel.

_____

_____

_____

_____

_____

_____

_____

_____

_____

GINGERBREAD for LIBERTY!

Prepare to Read

GENRE STUDY **Biographies** tell about real people's lives.

MAKE A PREDICTION Preview "An American Hero." Eleanor Roosevelt liked to help people. What do you think you will learn from reading this text?

_____

_____

_____

_____

_____

_____

SET A PURPOSE Read to find out why Eleanor Roosevelt is an important person in history.

An American Hero

READ As you read, think about what happened first, next, and last.

Eleanor Roosevelt was born in New York City in 1884. She was shy when she was little. When she was fifteen, she went to a boarding school in England. She was scared, but a kind teacher helped her. Soon Eleanor overcame her shyness.

In 1905, Eleanor married Franklin Roosevelt. Not long after, Franklin went into politics. Soon Eleanor began speaking up for things that were important to her, too. ▶

Close Reading Tip

Write **C** when you make a connection.

CHECK MY UNDERSTANDING

Which clues in the text tell you how the events are ordered?

_____

_____

READ As you read, answer the question, "What does this all mean to me?"

Close Reading Tip

Number the main events in order.

Then Franklin became president. Eleanor worked hard as the first lady. During wartime, Eleanor helped tend to the sick and hurt soldiers. She spoke out for all people in America to have the same rights. She also helped set rules for how people around the world should be treated. She thought this work was the best thing she did.

Sadly, Eleanor died in 1962. She will always be remembered for the change she brought to the world.

CHECK MY UNDERSTANDING

Why do you think Eleanor Roosevelt's accomplishments are an important part of American history?

_____

_____

_____

_____

WRITE ABOUT IT "An American Hero" tells what Eleanor Roosevelt did to help people around the world. What do you think people thought of Eleanor? Use details from the text to explain your answer.

_____

_____

_____

_____

_____

_____

_____

_____

_____

_____

Prepare to Read

GENRE STUDY **Realistic fiction** stories are made up but could happen in real life. As you read *Pepita and the Bully,* look for:

- characters who act and talk like real people
- events that could really happen
- setting in modern time in a place that could be real

SET A PURPOSE As you read, **retell** the story. Use your own words to tell what happened in the beginning, middle, and end of the story.

POWER WORDS

wrinkled

frown

yanked

dragged

mumbled

nearby

excuses

hesitant

Meet Ofelia Dumas Lachtman.

Pepita and Bully

and the

by Ofelia Dumas Lachtman

illustrated by Alex Pardo DeLange

Pepita waved goodbye to the bus driver. She raced down Pepper Street, her black braids bouncing behind her. She was in a hurry to get home and talk to Mamá. She wanted to tell her that three days in her new school were enough. She did not want to go there again.

Pepita's face wrinkled up into a big frown. She was sorry because she really liked Miss Chu, her teacher. Miss Chu had black eyes and a soft, sunny smile. Pepita also liked her classroom with bright bulletin boards and cut-out, red letters that said, "Welcome to a New School Year." She especially liked the playground with its tall shady tree and benches. But she did not like Babette. She had brown hair, blue eyes, and skin that looked like peach ice cream, but she was not nice.

Pepita's frown grew bigger when she remembered her first day of school. She had gone up to Babette and said, "Hello, my name's Pepita. What's yours?"

"Pepita, yuck," Babette said. "That's not a name. That's nothing but a noise."

Pepita felt her face grow hot. She was angry. "It is so a name," she said, "and it's mine!"

Babette just turned and walked away.

On the second day, Miss Chu asked her students to talk about their favorite things. Pepita told them her dog Lobo could understand Spanish.

At recess, Babette said, "I'll bet your dog has fleas."

Pepita felt her face grow hot. She was angry. "He does not!" she cried.

Babette just turned and walked away.

And today was even worse. Babette yanked her braids and said, "Your braids look like two raggedy ropes. You should cut them off."

Pepita felt her face grow hot. She was really angry. "They are *not* ropes," she cried. "They're braids! And if you pull them again, I'll tell Miss Chu!"

Babette yelled, "Tattletale, tattletale," and turned and walked away.

Pepita was glad when the school day was over. *Yes*, she thought as she raced home, *three days are enough. I don't want to go to that school again.*

In the middle of the block, Pepita saw Mrs. Green digging in her garden.

"Hello, Mrs. Green," she said, "Can I ask you something? Do you think my name is funny?"

"Why no, Pepita," Mrs. Green answered. "Your name has a very lovely sound. It reminds me of bright little flowers."

Pepita nodded and smiled. "That's nice," she said. "Thank you, Mrs. Green."

A few houses down the block, Pepita saw José, the mailman, stepping out of his truck.

"Hello, Señor José," she called. "Can I ask you something? Do you think Lobo understands Spanish?"

"Why, yes, Pepita, I do," the mailman answered. "I told him to sit. And when he did, I said, '*Buen perrito*. Good little dog,' and he wagged and wagged his tail. Of course he understands Spanish."

Pepita nodded and smiled. "I thought so, too," she said. "Thank you, Señor José."

When Pepita was near her own house, she saw Mrs. Becker standing by her easel, painting a pot of red geraniums.

"Hello, Mrs. Becker," she said. "Can I ask you something? Do you think my braids look like raggedy ropes?"

"Why, no, Pepita," Mrs. Becker answered. "Your braids are very lovely. They remind me of black satin ribbons shining in the sun."

Pepita nodded and smiled. "That's nice," she said. "Thank you, Mrs. Becker."

When Pepita got home, she found her mother in the kitchen.

"Mamá," she said, "I can't go back to that school again."

"Why?" Mamá asked. "I thought you liked your new school."

"So did I," Pepita said, "until I talked to Babette."

"And who is Babette?" Mamá asked.

"Babette is a bully," Pepita said. "She's mean to me, Mamá. I'm not going back to school."

"No, no," Mamá said, "that cannot be. School is important. But let's see what Papá has to say."

At supper that night, Pepita told her family what Babette had said to her. "She says my name is nothing but noise, that Lobo has fleas, and that my braids are raggedy ropes. And she yanked them! That's why I'm not going back to school!"

"I see," Papá said, "but you have to go to school. So tomorrow if Babette yanks your braids again, you must tell your teacher. But if Babette says mean things to you, either you can answer her politely or you can walk away. But whatever you do, you must be kind."

"Kind?" Pepita asked. "Is that like *nice*?"

Papá nodded. "Yes, *nice* will do."

Pepita's brother Juan said, "Just don't fight with her. Bullies like fights."

In bed Pepita tossed and turned and tumbled until her blankets were in a tangle. She dragged her doll Dora out from under the blankets and placed her against the pillow. "Dora," she said, "tomorrow Babette will say mean things to me."

Dora's face looked sad.

Pepita sat up straight and punched the pillow. "What if she tries to hit me?!"

Dora disappeared under the blankets.

Pepita pulled her out again. "Don't worry, Dora," she said, "I'll think of something." Dora huddled close. They snuggled together and fell asleep.

In the morning, Pepita got out of bed slowly. She dressed slowly. She ate breakfast slowly. She twisted and turned and muttered and mumbled while Mamá brushed and braided her hair. But no matter what Pepita did, nothing slowed down the clock. It was time to go to school.

"Mamá," Pepita complained, "three days are enough."

But Mamá said, "School is important, and if you don't hurry, you'll be late."

So Pepita went to school. Her classroom was sunny and bright. Her teacher smiled at her. But across the room Babette wrinkled up her nose and made an ugly face. At recess Mindy asked Pepita to play hopscotch. Pepita was about to say yes, but she saw Babette standing nearby. She gave Mindy a friendly wave, went to the farthest corner of the playground and sat under the shady tree. Babette was right behind her.

"That's my bench," Babette said. "I don't like you sitting there."

Pepita stood up. "What *do* you like?" she asked, and started to walk away.

"I don't like you for sure," Babette said.

Pepita felt her face grow hot. She was angry. She stopped and turned. "Maybe you don't like anything at all," she called.

"Maybe you don't even like your name. *Maybe you don't even like yourself.* And I'll bet you don't even have a dog!"

"You aren't nice," Babette said, and a tear rolled down her cheek. "You aren't nice at all."

Pepita's mouth dropped wide open. Her brother had told her not to fight. Papá had told her to be kind. And look what she had done! Babette was crying!

"Most times I'm nice," Pepita said, "and I'm polite, too. But you say mean things. Maybe if you stop being mean, somebody would ask you to play, too."

"I wouldn't play if you were playing because I don't like your braids," Babette said.

"See? You're being mean."

"I wouldn't play if you were playing because you have a funny name," Babette said.

"You're just being mean again. Anyway, Pepita's who I am."

"But I might play," Babette said, "if . . ."

"Stop making excuses!" Pepita said. "Do you want to play or don't you?"

Babette bit her lip, sniffed and gave a hesitant little nod.

"Okay," Pepita said, "but you'd better blow your nose."

She handed Babette a tissue from her pocket. Then she swung around and raced toward the center of the yard. "Wait, Mindy! Wait for us! Babette and I want to play!"

Turn and Talk

Use details from *Pepita and the Bully* to answer these questions with a partner.

1. **Retell** Take turns telling the story events in order. Use order words such as *first, next, after,* and *at the end* to help you.

2. Who is telling the story? Why do you think the author chose this point of view?

3. Papá tells Pepita to be kind. What do you think of this advice? Find details in the text and pictures that show how Pepita feels about it.

Talking Tip

Ask to learn more about one of your partner's ideas. Complete the sentence below.

Please tell me more about _____ .

Write a Letter

PROMPT What should Babette say to apologize to Pepita? Look for details in the text and pictures that tell what Babette did and how it made Pepita feel.

PLAN First, write notes about the things Babette should apologize for.

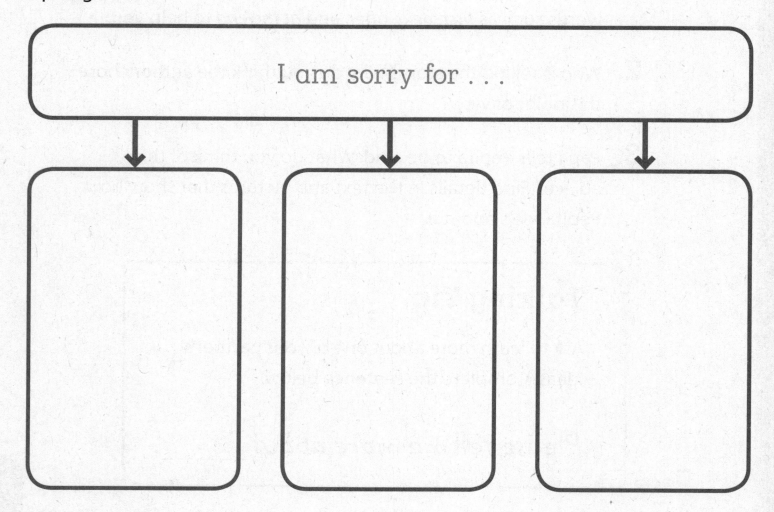

I am sorry for . . .

WRITE Now help Babette apologize! Write an apology letter from Babette to Pepita. Remember to:

- Use the word *because* to explain why Babette is sorry.

- Begin your letter with *Dear Pepita*. End the letter with *Your friend, Babette.*

_____

_____

_____

_____

_____

_____

_____

_____

_____

Prepare to Read

GENRE STUDY **Realistic fiction** stories are made up but could happen in real life.

MAKE A PREDICTION Preview "More Than One Way to Win." Alex and Maya are the fastest runners in the school. What do you think will happen when they have a disagreement?

_____

_____

_____

_____

_____

_____

SET A PURPOSE Read to find out what lesson the characters in the story learn.

More Than One Way to Win

READ What happens at the beginning of the story? <u>Underline</u> the reason Maya gets angry.

Maya and Alex are the fastest runners in school. They are friends, but they are always trying to beat each other on the track. One day, Maya hears Alex telling some friends that he just lets her win sometimes. Maya gets mad. She knows she shouldn't, but she says something mean to Alex. Now they aren't getting along. They decide to settle their disagreement with a race.

> **Close Reading Tip**
>
> Number the main events in order.

CHECK MY UNDERSTANDING

What have you learned about Alex and Maya?

_____

_____

_____

READ What is this part of the story mostly about?

Close Reading Tip

Put a **!** by a surprising part.

The race begins. Maya and Alex are tied the whole way. Then, Alex suddenly falls. Maya has to make a decision. Should she keep running or stop to help?

"I'm fine," Alex grunts, rubbing his ankle. "You go on."

"Don't be silly," Maya says as she pulls him up.

Then, leaning against each other, they hobble toward the finish line together.

Maya smiles. "I'm sorry we had a disagreement, Alex."

"I'm sorry, too. Maybe we should run relays together instead of racing against each other!" Alex suggests.

"Count me in. We make a great team!" Maya says.

CHECK MY UNDERSTANDING

What lesson do Maya and Alex learn?

_____

_____

_____

WRITE ABOUT IT Retell the story in your own words. Use details from the story to tell what happens in the beginning, the middle, and the end.

_____

_____

_____

_____

_____

_____

_____

_____

_____

_____

Prepare to Read

GENRE STUDY **Infographics** give information quickly and in a visual way. As you read *Be a Hero! Work It Out!,* notice:

- the purpose of the infographic
- how pictures, symbols, and words work together
- words or phrases that stand out
- what the author wants you to learn

SET A PURPOSE Think about the infographic's **central idea.** How do the words, numbers, and symbols work together to help you understand the infographic's purpose?

Build Background: Bullying

BE A HERO!
Work It Out!
by Ruben Cooley

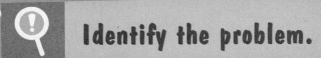 Identify the problem.

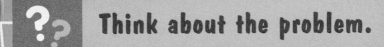 Think about the problem.

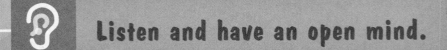 Attack the problem, not the person.

 Listen and have an open mind.

Be respectful of feelings.

 Know that everyone makes mistakes—own up to yours.

Knock out these enemies: Hitting Making threats Pushing Name-calling Making excuses Not listening Making mean faces Bullying

Hello, citizens!

Captain Problem Solver here!

I have been told there are some problems on the streets. Some kids don't know how to solve problems. No, not *math* problems—problems with each other. I need your help spreading the word about my tips!

SCHOOL

Let's break these down a little. When you are sharing my tips, these are three important ones to start with. When there is a problem, kids should first identify that there is a problem. People don't agree all the time. So they should think about what the problem is before doing anything. Remember to attack the problem, not the person. That would just make the problem worse!

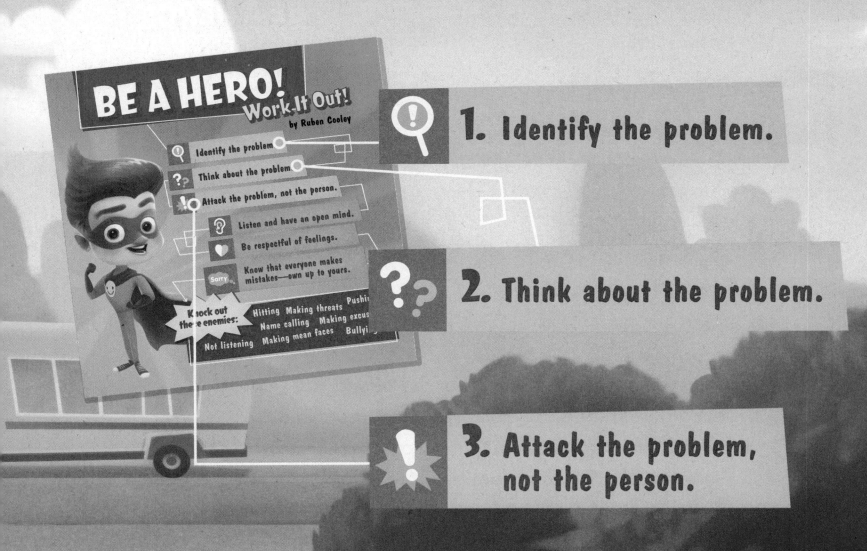

BE A HERO!
Work It Out!
by Ruben Cooley

- Identify the problem
- Think about the problem.
- Attack the problem, not the person.

- Listen and have an open mind.
- Be respectful of feelings.
- Know that everyone makes mistakes—own up to yours.

Knock out these enemies: Hitting Making threats Pushin
Name calling Making excus
Not listening Making mean faces Bullyi

1. Identify the problem.

2. Think about the problem.

3. Attack the problem, not the person.

So what can kids do?

Share the next three tips!

 4. Listen and have an open mind.

 5. Be respectful of feelings.

 **6.** Know that everyone makes mistakes—own up to yours.

Kids should listen to each other. Someone else might have a different idea of what happened. It could be just a misunderstanding. Listening to each other also shows that the other person's feelings are being respected. Knowing someone cares about your feelings makes you feel better, right? It can help with problem solving, too!

Finally, owning up to mistakes is part of life. As you share my tips with other kids, make sure you know this one well. Practice it yourself! Everyone can make mistakes, and admitting you have made one can be hard. It makes you a brave citizen to admit you have made one!

Hitting

Bullying

Making threats

Name-calling

Pushing

Not listening

Making excuses

Making mean faces

These are the enemies that can stop kids from solving a problem and make the problem worse. Look for them every day and help stop them!

My work here is done. Thank you for sharing my tips about problem solving, citizens! I know with your help, we will have more citizens on the streets being problem solvers!

Be a problem solver superhero like me!

Use details from *Be a Hero! Work It Out!* to answer these questions with a partner.

1. **Central Idea** What is the hero's message? Which details in the text help you figure out the central idea?

2. How do the numbers, symbols, and words help you understand what the hero is trying to persuade you to do?

3. The hero says that it is brave to own up to your mistakes. Think about a time you made a mistake. How does that help you understand what the hero means?

Talking Tip

Complete the sentence to ask your partner for more information about an answer.

Tell me more about _____.

Let's Wrap Up!

? Essential Question

How can people work out disagreements?

Pick one of these activities to show what you have learned about the topic.

1. Sing It Out

Make up a song about what to do when a problem comes along. Look back at the texts for ideas about how to resolve a conflict. Share your song with the class.

> **Word Challenge**
> Can you use the word **compromise** in your song?

2. Make a Glossary

Find words in the texts that tell about solving problems. Make a list of at least five words. Then put them in ABC order. Write the meaning of each word next to the word.

My Notes

Once Upon a Time

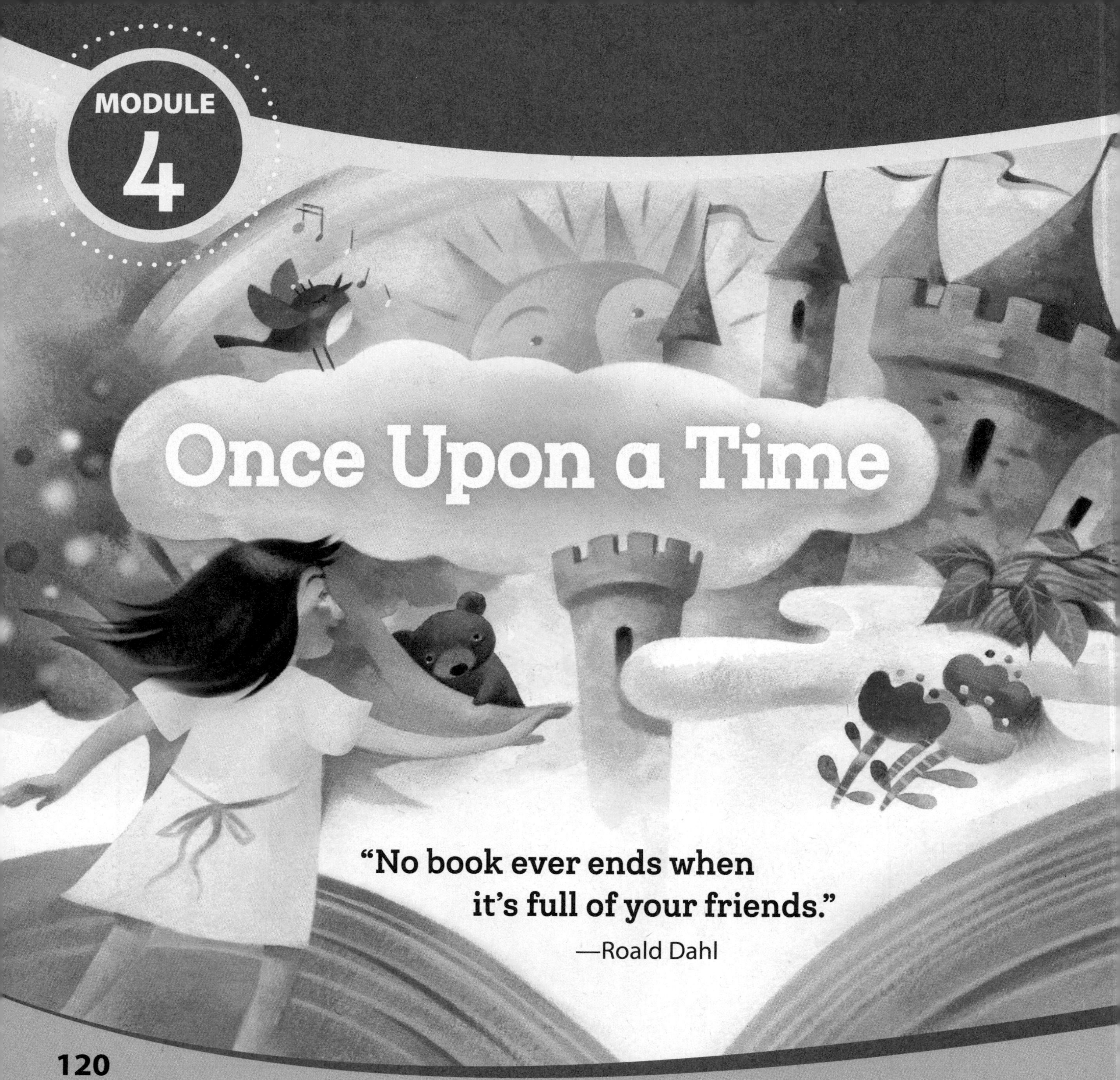

"No book ever ends when
it's full of your friends."
—Roald Dahl

? Essential Question

What lessons can we learn from the characters in stories?

Get Curious Video

Words About Storytelling

Complete the Vocabulary Network to show what you know about the words.

moral	
Meaning: A **moral** is a lesson in a story.	
Synonyms and Antonyms	Drawing

relate

Meaning: If you **relate** to someone, you know how the person feels.

Synonyms and Antonyms	Drawing

version

Meaning: A **version** is a different or changed form of something.

Synonyms and Antonyms	Drawing

Recipe for a Fairy Tale

You can use a recipe to make breakfast, lunch, or dinner. Can you use one to make a fairy tale, too? Let's find out!

Ingredients

prince

princess

dragon

castle

golden eggs

picnic basket

Directions

1. First, let's do some mixing.

2. Take the castle and the dragon.

3. Add a prince, a princess, and a picnic basket.

4. Now, sprinkle in a little bit of silliness.

5. Stir them all together. What have you got? Read on to find out!

The Story

Once upon a time, a dragon lived all alone in a castle. He never came out or opened the door. The villagers thought he was mean.

One day, a brave prince and a daring princess decided to save their frightened kingdom from the dragon. They marched up to the castle door. The prince hollered, "Open this door, or I'll huff and puff and blow your house down!"

The dragon was very surprised. He peeked out a window and asked, "Really? What if I **do** open the door?"

The princess held up a picnic basket. "Then we can have lunch," she said.

The lonely dragon opened the door. He invited his new friends in for lunch. They all lived happily ever after.

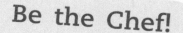

Be the Chef!
What would you mix up for a fairy tale?

Prepare to Read

GENRE STUDY **Procedural texts** tell readers how to do or make something. When you read *How to Read a Story*, notice:

- directions for readers to follow
- main topic and details
- steps that show order
- ways visuals and words help readers understand the text

SET A PURPOSE Read to make smart guesses, or **inferences,** about things the author does not say. Use clues in the text and pictures to help you.

POWER WORDS

cozy
steaming
clue
sense
pause
disturb
rattled
tackled

Meet Kate Messner.

HOW TO
READ
A STORY

by Kate Messner

illustrated by Mark Siegel

STEP 1

FIND A STORY.

A good one.
It can have princesses and castles,
if you like that sort of thing,
or witches and trolls.
(As long as they're not too scary.)

STEP 2

FIND A READING BUDDY.

A good one.

A buddy can be older . . .

or younger . . .

or a person your age.

Or maybe not a person at all.

Make sure your reading buddy is nice and snuggly.
And make sure you both like the book.
If you don't agree . . . go back to Step 1.
Sometimes it takes a few tries to find just the right book.

STEP 3

FIND A COZY READING SPOT.

Outside is fun . . . but not if it's very cold.
Unless you have thick woolen blankets,
and hats and scarves, and cups of steaming
hot cocoa.

And not if it's very hot.
Unless you have trees to shade you from
the sun, a hammock to catch cool
breezes, and tall glasses of icy lemonade.

Inside is good.
Couches are cozy. So are chairs
big enough for two.

Just be careful not to get stuck.

STEP 4

LOOK AT THE BOOK'S COVER.

Can you guess what it's about?
Read the title. That might be a clue.

STEP 5

OPEN THE BOOK.

(This is the exciting part!)

Read the story in a loud, clear voice,
not too slow and not too fast.

You can point to words if you like,
but you don't have to do that.

"Once upon a time ..."

STEP 6

When the characters talk,
whatever's being said . . .
say it in a voice to match who's talking.

"I will save the kingdom."

"I am the most POWERFUL
in all the land!"

"Soon the castle
will be MINE."

"I'm hungry
for lunch."

"Beep."

STEP 7

No matter what you read, hold the book so your buddy can see the pictures. Buddies get impatient when they can't see well.

STEP 8

If there are words you don't know, try sounding them out or looking at the pictures to see what makes sense.

"They were afraid the dragon would burn down the cass . . . cass . . . Oh . . . The castle!"

They were afraid the dragon would burn down castle.

If you need a break, you can pause for a minute . . .
and talk to your reading buddy
to predict what might happen next.

Will the castle catch on fire?
Will the princess tame the dragon?
Will the robot marry the princess?
Will the horse make friends with the dragon?
Will the dragon eat them all for lunch?

STEP 9

When you get to the exciting parts,
make your voice sound exciting, too.

"Who dares disturb me in my cave?" the dragon growled.

"Oh dear! Oh no!"
The robot was so scared all his metal
parts rattled. What would they do?

But the princess tackled that
dragon and held him down.

"You must promise you'll
leave our kingdom in peace!"

140

When you and your buddy can't stand it a second longer . . .

turn the page to read
how things work out.

STEP 10

When the book is over, say,

"The End."

And then . . . if it was a really good story . . .
go right back to the beginning
and start all over again.

Turn and Talk

Use details from *How to Read a Story* to answer these questions with a partner.

1. **Make Inferences** Why is it important to find just the right book for you and your reading buddy?

2. How are the numbered steps in the text connected? What does the author want you to learn from them?

3. How do you think the author feels about reading? How do you think she wants others to feel about it? Use details from the text to explain your ideas.

Talking Tip

Your ideas are important! Be sure to speak loudly and clearly as you share them.

Write More Steps

PROMPT Think about how following the steps in *How to Read a Story* can help make reading fun. Now think about what makes reading fun for you. What other steps could you add to the text?

PLAN First, draw two steps that you would like to share with others. Be sure they are different from the steps in the text.

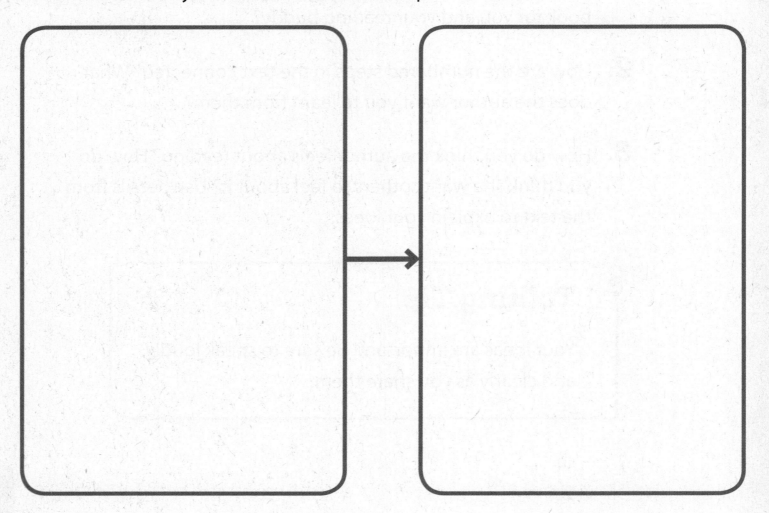

WRITE Now write your own steps to add to *How to Read a Story*. Remember to:

- Choose verbs that tell your readers exactly what to do.

- Use language that will make readers excited about following your steps.

_____

_____

_____

_____

_____

_____

_____

_____

Prepare to Read

GENRE STUDY ▸ **Procedural texts** explain to readers how to make or do something.

MAKE A PREDICTION ▸ Preview "How to Find a Story." Look at the features, like the numbers and bold text. What do you think you will read about?

_____

_____

_____

_____

_____

SET A PURPOSE ▸ Read to learn how to find a story and to see if your prediction is right. If not, think about the text and look carefully at the features. Then make a new prediction.

How to Find a Story

READ Why might beginning to write a story be a little scary?

What do all writers have in common? They all begin with a blank piece of paper. A blank piece of paper can be exciting! It is full of possibilities. Just think of all the stories that have come to life on a piece of paper. That blank paper can be a little bit scary, too. How is it going to be filled?

Close Reading Tip
Write **C** when you make a connection.

One way to get ideas is to read, read, READ. Most writers read a lot. They study how *their* favorite writers create characters and describe events. They think about the ingredients for a great story.

What other things can writers do to help them create? ▶

READ How are the steps in this list connected?

These steps will help you think of ideas to write about.

1. **Be curious!** Ideas are everywhere. Look and listen wherever you go.

2. **Write notes.** Keep a notebook with you. Write and make sketches about the ideas you find.

3. **Take risks!** An idea might seem wild or wacky now, but it can turn into something wonderful. Don't be afraid to make mistakes. That is how you learn!

4. **Write every day.** Use the ideas in your notebook. Maybe you write a little bit. Maybe you write a lot. See where your ideas take you.

When it's time to fill that blank page, you will be ready!

CHECK MY UNDERSTANDING

What is the author's purpose for writing this text? Why does the author include a numbered list?

_____

_____

_____

_____

WRITE ABOUT IT   Read the steps carefully. What other steps could help writers find and grow their ideas? Write two more steps that you would add to the author's list. Be sure to think about the order of the steps. Where do your new steps fit in?

_____

_____

_____

_____

_____

_____

_____

_____

_____

_____

_____

_____

Prepare to Read

GENRE STUDY **Dramas** are plays that are read and performed. As you read *A Crow, a Lion, and a Mouse! Oh, My!,* look for:

- the setting, or where and when the story takes place
- a narrator who reads words the characters do not say
- a list of characters

SET A PURPOSE As you read, **create mental images,** or make pictures in your mind, to help you understand details in the text.

POWER WORDS

plain

bind

narrow

clever

Meet Crystal Hubbard.

A Crow, a Lion, and a Mouse! Oh, My!

two fables retold by Crystal Hubbard

The Lion and the Mouse

CAST: NARRATOR
LION
MOUSE
HUNTER 1
HUNTER 2

NARRATOR On a sunny plain in Kenya, Lion sleeps.

LION *Snooooore!*

MOUSE *(enters, noisily talking on cell phone)* Have you tasted the new cheeses at the Nairobi Food Mart? They're so good, and they're on sale!

LION *(wakes, grabs Mouse)* I don't like cheeses. I prefer to snack on *meeses!* I mean mice.

MOUSE *(looking fearful)* Please, don't eat me! I'm not even a mouthful. I'm more useful outside your belly than inside.

LION *(yawns)* I'm more sleepy than hungry anyway. Run along, little Mouse. *(falls asleep)*

NARRATOR Sleeping Lion cannot hear danger approach.

HUNTER 1 (carrying a rope, whispers) This lion will be our greatest prize!

HUNTER 2 (helps Hunter 1 bind surprised Lion) Let's get the truck!

NARRATOR Mighty Lion has a mighty big problem!

MOUSE (nibbling cheese, drops cheese when he sees Lion) Dude, what happened?

LION (looking ashamed) Hunters trapped me. I'm so embarrassed!

MOUSE Not for long!

NARRATOR Mouse's tiny, sharp teeth chewed and gnawed and tugged at the rope until it fell away.

LION I'm free! (hugs Mouse) I learned a lesson today. You're a better friend than a meal! (Smiling, Lion and Mouse exit together.)

The Crow and the Pitcher

CAST: CROW 1
CROW 2
NARRATOR

NARRATOR On the hottest day of summer, two crows find a pitcher of water.

CROW 1 *(circling pitcher)* It's half full!

CROW 2 *(wings crossed over chest)* It's half empty.

CROW 1 *(tries to stick beak in pitcher)* The opening is too narrow!

CROW 2 *(tries to lift pitcher)* I can't hold it because I don't have thumbs!

NARRATOR The crows grow thirstier in the heat of the sizzling sun.

CROW 1 *(staring at pitcher)* There has to be a way to get that water.

CROW 2 *(kicking pebble on ground)* I wish I had ice cream. *(kicks a pebble)* Or an ice pop. *(kicks a pebble)*

CROW 1 I've got it! *(picks up a pebble)*

CROW 2 What are you doing with that?

CROW 1 *(drops pebble into pitcher)* You'll see.

157

CROW 2 Are you making Pebble-ade?

CROW 1 *(picks up pebble, drops it in pitcher)*
Just keep watching and you'll see how smart I am!

NARRATOR This clever crow can't get to the water, so he's making the water get to him.

CROW 2 *(impressed)* Wow! The water is rising!

CROW 1 *(spits out pebble)* It would rise faster if both of us put in pebbles. *(picks up pebble)*

CROW 2 No, that's okay. You're doing great.

CROW 1 *(drops pebble in pitcher)* There! I can finally get a drink. *(begins sipping water)*

CROW 2 *(behind Crow 1)* Hurry, I want a turn! Save some for me!

Use details from *A Crow, a Lion, and a Mouse! Oh, My!* to answer these questions with a partner.

1. **Create Mental Images** When Mouse sees what happened to Lion, he is so surprised he drops his cheese. What does Mouse see? Use details in the text to help you picture it in your mind. Then describe your picture to a partner.

2. How is the narrator's part different from the other parts in each drama?

3. Why is a fable a good way to teach a lesson? What lessons do you learn from these two fables?

Listening Tip

Look at your partner as you listen. Nod your head to show you are interested.

Write a Thank-You Note

PROMPT How do you think Lion feels about what Mouse did to help him? Use details from the words and pictures to explain your ideas.

PLAN First, add words to the web that describe how you think Lion feels after Mouse helps him.

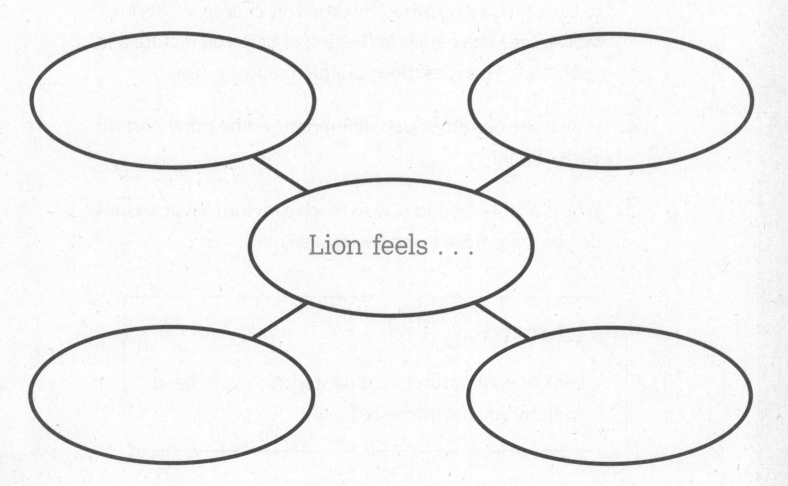

Lion feels . . .

WRITE Now write a note from Lion to Mouse thanking him for his help. Remember to:

- Include details from the drama that explain why Lion is thanking Mouse.

- Begin your note with *Dear Mouse*. End it with *Your friend, Lion*.

_____

_____

_____

_____

_____

_____

_____

_____

_____

Prepare to Read

GENRE STUDY **Dramas** are plays that are read and performed.

MAKE A PREDICTION Preview "The Wind and the Sun." Wind and Sun disagree. You know that dramas have characters, dialogue, and a setting. What do you think this drama will be about?

_____

_____

_____

_____

_____

_____

_____

SET A PURPOSE Read to find out how Wind and Sun decide to settle their disagreement.

The Wind and the Sun

READ Circle words that create a picture in your mind.

Cast of Characters: Bob, Narrator, Sun, Wind
Setting: a cool spring day in the country

NARRATOR: Up in the sky, a disagreement is beginning.

WIND: I don't mean to brag, but I am the very most powerful force in the universe.

SUN: I disagree, my friend. My power is greater.

WIND: No way! Think about it. I can twist myself into a giant tornado if I want to.

SUN: Yes, but my warmth and light can make tiny seeds grow into mighty trees.

WIND: Let's settle this once and for all.

NARRATOR: Just then, they saw a man taking a walk. He was wearing a warm, woolly coat. ▶

Close Reading Tip
Underline words that tell about the setting.

163

READ How do stage directions tell more about the characters?

SUN: How about this? Whoever can get Bob to take his coat off is the winner.

WIND: Oh boy, this is going to be so easy. *(blowing)* Whoosh!

NARRATOR: Bob shivers a little bit.

WIND: *(blowing harder)* Whoosh! Whooosh! Whoooooosh!

BOB: My, it sure is windy. I better button up. *Brrrr!*

SUN: Let me give it a try. I will turn up my heat and SHINE!

NARRATOR: Bob smiles and takes off his coat.

BOB: Wow, that sun feels great. What a funny day.

WIND: Sunny, you won this fair and square. I think I've learned a lesson, my friend.

SUN: *(smiling)* Being gentle is a very great power.

Close Reading Tip

Underline the lesson that Wind learns.

CHECK MY UNDERSTANDING

How is the setting an important part of this drama?

_____

_____

_____

_____

WRITE ABOUT IT How would Bob tell the story? Write the events in order the way Bob would tell them. Describe what Bob was thinking, feeling, and doing on his walk.

_____

_____

_____

_____

_____

_____

_____

_____

_____

_____

Prepare to Read

GENRE STUDY ▶ **Fantasies** are stories with events that could not really happen. As you read *Hollywood Chicken,* look for:

- animal characters that talk and act like real people
- the beginning, middle, and ending of the story
- problems and solutions

SET A PURPOSE ▶ You know that most stories include a problem. Use what you know about the text to make a **prediction,** or good guess, about the problem in this story. Read to see if you are right. If not, make a new prediction.

POWER WORDS

journey
fulfill
believe
speech

Build Background: Hollywood

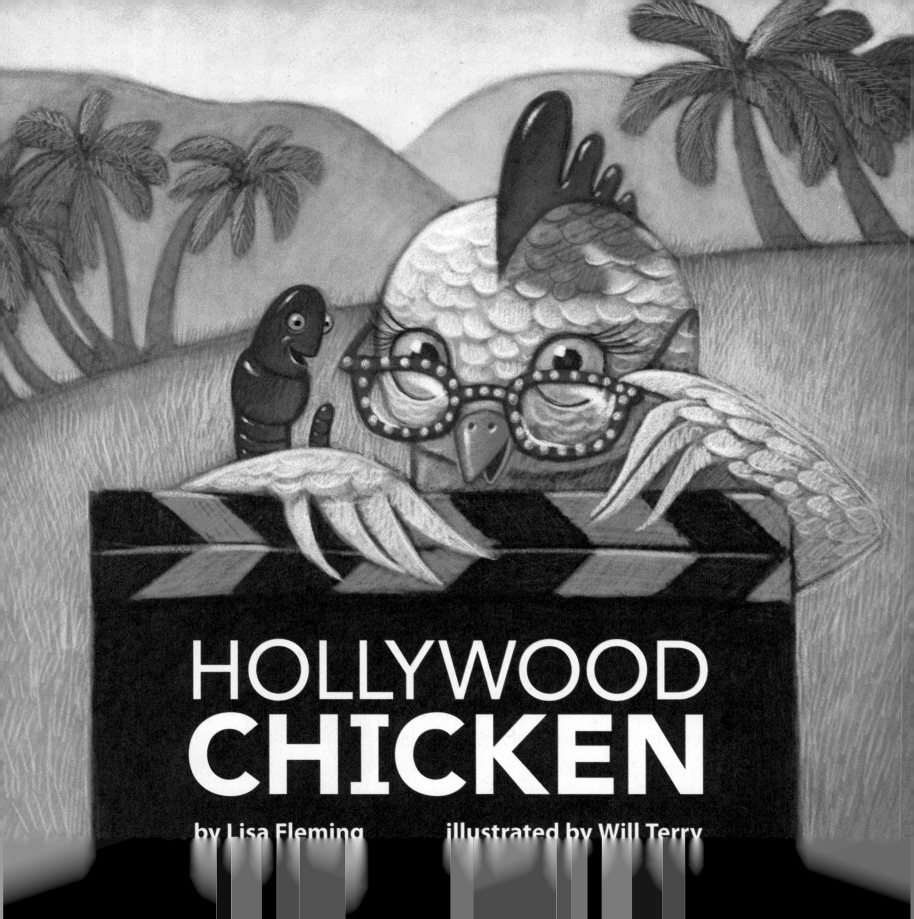

HOLLYWOOD
CHICKEN

by Lisa Fleming   illustrated by Will Terry

Dear Ms. Luz Cruz,

   I can't wait to fly this coop! Life in these green hills is dull, dull, dull. The endless farmland, quiet evenings, and the steady diet of corn and more corn just aren't enough for me. I need more from life! How I dream of being on stage! I want to make my way in the city where dreams come true! I could be the next poultry actress to make it big! I, Chicken Lily, will have my own star on the Hollywood Chicken Walk of Fame! Hollywood, here I come!

Sincerely,
Chicken Lily

Dear Chicken Lily,
   I am excited to meet you! I am Hollywood's best chicken agent. I will get you parts in movies and help you dream big. I can see your name in lights already! Call me or text me when you get here! 323-555-BOCK
                                          Kisses,
                                          Luz Cruz

Ms. Cruz, it's Chicken Lily. I did it! I'm here in Hollywood! My journey was long. I went from the wide green fields of home, over mountains, and through deserts. I had a rough time crossing through the tiny towns filled with homes and cars and people. There was a close call with a cat in Burbank, but I made it!

Oh, the city! It's everything I dreamed it would be! It's big, busy, and beautiful! The buildings are so tall. There are so many people. The noise of the city is so different than the quiet of my home on the farm.

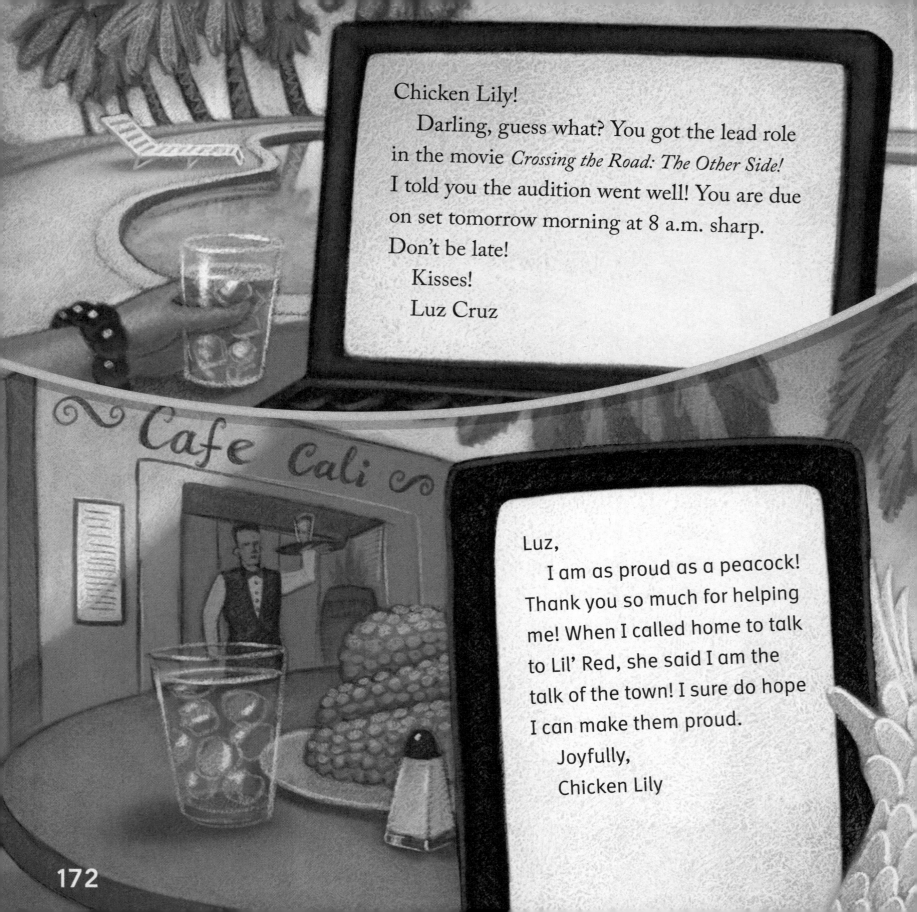

Chicken Lily!

Darling, guess what? You got the lead role in the movie *Crossing the Road: The Other Side!* I told you the audition went well! You are due on set tomorrow morning at 8 a.m. sharp. Don't be late!

Kisses!

Luz Cruz

Luz,

I am as proud as a peacock! Thank you so much for helping me! When I called home to talk to Lil' Red, she said I am the talk of the town! I sure do hope I can make them proud.

Joyfully,

Chicken Lily

Dear Chicken Diary,

Today I got to meet the other actors on my movie. So many of them have gone to big chicken acting schools. A lot have come from families where the chickens all work in the movies. What if I don't fit in?

One of the actors sure made me feel like I don't belong. Slim the Worm made a joke about the way I talk. He didn't think I heard him, but I did.

Did I make the wrong decision when I left the farm? What if I can't fulfill my dream? Maybe I should let Luz Cruz know there is a problem on the set. I don't want her to think I'm as helpless as a chick, though.

Dear Chicken Diary,

    Who would believe it? *Crossing the Road: The Other Side* is a smash hit! The movie's success has made me want to work even harder. I started taking a chicken acting class. Every day I meet with my friends to practice my acting skills. I think it is paying off. We start filming *Crossing the Road 2: The Highway* tomorrow!

One thing still bothers me: Slim. He never talks to me on the set. I try to be friendly, but he is always joking around in a way that hurts my feelings. Does he think that I don't belong here? I did talk to Luz about it. She said, "Just talk to him, Chicken Lily! I've worked with him for a long time. You might be worrying about nothing!" I want to talk to him. I'm just scared!

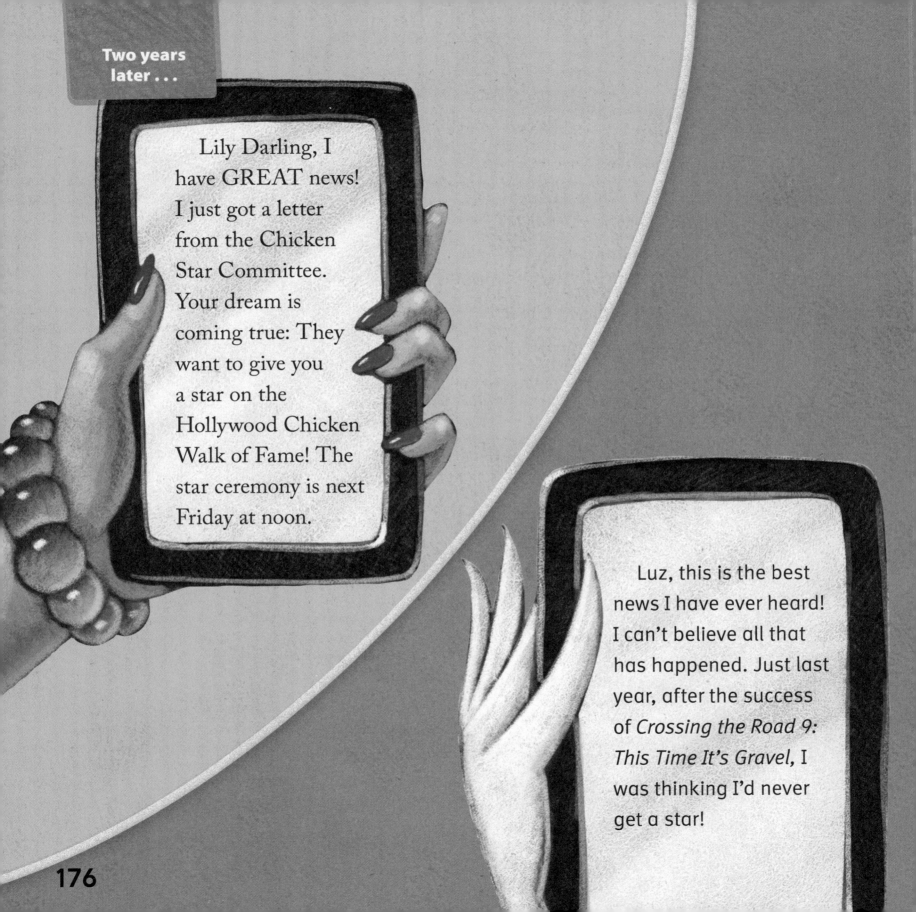

Dear Chicken Diary,

Today was the star ceremony, and it was amazing! I got to give a speech! I also left my chicken footprints in the wet cement on my very own star. My dream came true!

All of my friends from the *Crossing the Road* movies were there. Well, all of them were there except Slim.

Dear Chicken Diary,

On my way home, I saw Slim sitting alone on a park bench. I took a chance and asked him what was wrong. He seemed so surprised that I had asked.

"Sometimes I feel like I don't belong," Slim told me. "I make jokes when I'm nervous, and I know I hurt others' feelings. It's just that I want so much to be a good actor, but all I ever get are small parts. My career will never get off the ground." I was very glad I took Luz's advice to talk to him!

I put my arm around Slim and told him my story. I told him about my journey from the farm and how I had wondered if I would ever fit in. I told him about my years and years of practice and hard work. And I told him that I would help him make his dreams come true. Maybe some day, my friend Slim might be the first worm to have a star on the Hollywood Chicken Walk of Fame.

Turn and Talk

HOLLYWOOD
CHICKEN

Use details from *Hollywood Chicken* to answer these questions with a partner.

1. **Make and Confirm Predictions** What predictions did you make about the problem and resolution before and as you read? What were you right about? What was different?

2. How do the places where Lily lives change in the story? What clues do you see in the pictures about her success?

3. How does Lily feel when she talks to Slim at the end of the story? How does she show her feelings?

Listening Tip

Listen carefully and politely. Look at your partner to show you are paying attention.

Write a Movie Ad

PROMPT Movie ads use words and pictures to get people excited about seeing a movie. What would a movie ad for *Crossing the Road: The Other Side* be like? Look for details in the words and pictures to help you think of ideas.

PLAN First, think of an exciting scene that might be in the movie. Draw it. Add the title and the names of the stars.

WRITE Now ask yourself what would make you want to see this movie. Write sentences that would persuade other kids to want to see it, too. Remember to:

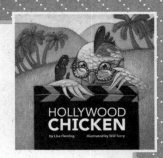

- Include details about the movie's stars and setting.

- Use describing words such as *greatest*, *silliest*, and *stupendous*.

_____

_____

_____

_____

_____

_____

_____

_____

_____

Prepare to Read

GENRE STUDY **Fantasies** are stories with made-up events that could not really happen.

MAKE A PREDICTION Preview "The Best View." Two friends disagree about where to view a sunset. You know that a fantasy has make-believe events. What do you think will happen in this story?

_____

_____

_____

_____

_____

_____

SET A PURPOSE Read to understand a lesson learned by one of the characters and to see if your prediction is right. If not, think about what a fantasy story is like and make a new prediction.

The Best View

READ <u>Underline</u> two similes. How do they make the story interesting to read?

One summer evening, Hal and Joy decided to watch the sunset. They climbed a tall tree. It was a lovely, peaceful spot.

"The view is like a dream," Joy sighed. "It reminds me of my favorite poem. It goes…"

CLICK! Hal took a picture with his phone. He looked at the screen and frowned. "I don't think this is the best view," he said. "Let's try a taller tree."

"OK, but we have to run like the wind," Joy said. "It's almost sunset time."

She and Hal climbed an even taller tree with an even prettier view.

Close Reading Tip
Mark the characters' opinions with a *.

READ What words help you picture the sunset? <u>Underline</u> them.

Close Reading Tip

Put a ! by a surprising part.

"Look how that fiery orange sun reflects on the shimmery water," Joy began. "It looks like…"

CLICK! Hal took another photo, looked at his screen, and frowned again. "Can you believe it? That bird just photobombed my sunset."

"Put that away," Joy groaned. "You are missing a stunning sunset!" But it was too late. The sun went down. Hal felt blue.

"Don't worry," Joy said. "We can come back tomorrow and watch the sunrise."

The next morning, Hal left his phone at home. He and Joy watched a beautiful sunrise together. It was as pretty as a picture.

CHECK MY UNDERSTANDING

Think about the predictions you made before and during reading. Were they correct? Tell why or why not.

_____

_____

_____

WRITE ABOUT IT What lesson does Hal learn? Use details
from the text to explain your answer.

_____

_____

_____

_____

_____

_____

_____

_____

_____

_____

Prepare to Read

GENRE STUDY **Fairy tales** are old stories with made-up characters and events that could not happen. As you read *If the Shoe Fits: Two Cinderella Stories*, look for:

- clues that the stories are make-believe
- endings that are happy
- problems and solutions

SET A PURPOSE As you read, **make connections** by finding ways that this text is like things in your life and other texts you have read. This will help you understand and remember the text.

POWER WORDS

chore

thrilled

superb

beamed

pleasure

jealous

dashed

hobbled

Meet Pleasant DeSpain.

If the Shoe Fits

Two Cinderella Stories

retold by Pleasant DeSpain

A Cinderella Named Zoey

Once, not long ago, there was a girl named Zoey. She loved school, especially math, PE, and science.

Her stepbrother, Finn, enjoyed playing tricks on Zoey.

One day, their mother tried logging onto her laptop, but her password wasn't accepted.

"Finn, did you change my password?"

"No, Mom. Try Zoey's password."

It worked.

"Zoey!" cried their mother. "You know the rule. You can't use my computer without permission. Instead of going to Randall's party tomorrow, you'll do Finn's chore and mow the lawn."

"But Mom, I didn't . . ."

Laughing, Finn went outside.

Randall had invited all his friends to his birthday party. His mom was baking a delicious chocolate cake. He hoped Zoey would come. She was one of his best friends.

The next day, Finn and their mom left for Randall's party.

The doorbell rang. It was Zoey's favorite neighbor, Mrs. Fortuna. She always sparkled!

"Want to go to the party?"

"How did you know?"

"I have a few secrets, dear."

"But the lawn . . ." began Zoey.

Mrs. Fortuna pulled bright red garden shears from her bag. To Zoey's amazement, the shears flew out of Mrs. Fortuna's hands. The lawn was mowed in seconds.

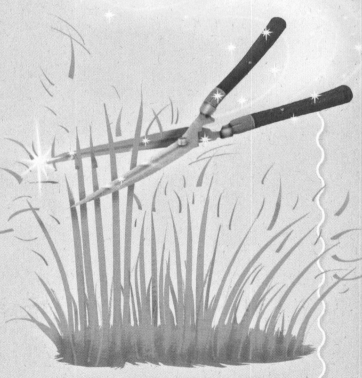

Zoey was thrilled! She ran to get her favorite shoes, but Finn had hidden them.

"What will I wear?"

Mrs. Fortuna handed her a pair of golden tennis shoes. Zoey thought they were superb!

On the way to Randall's house, one of Zoey's shoes came untied and tumbled onto the street. It was run over by a bus.

"My shoe!" yelled Zoey.

Mrs. Fortuna consoled her. "Two shoes don't make wishes come true."

Randall beamed when Zoey walked in. He invited her to sit next to him. Noticing her one shoe, he thought, "This is something new." Then he said, "Cool, everyone take off one shoe, just like Zoey."

It was time to cut the cake. The candles were lit, and before Randall blew them out, Zoey smiled. One of her wishes had come true.

A Cinderella Named Kwan

A Korean Story

Long, long ago, a baby girl was born. Her father named her Kwan, which means "strong."

Sadly, her mother died.

Years later, Kwan's father remarried. His new wife had her own daughter named Hee, which means "pleasure."

Kwan's stepmother and stepsister were jealous of Kwan and unkind to her.

One beautiful spring morning, Kwan's stepmother said, "I'm taking Hee to the festival."

"Can I go, honorable mother?" asked Kwan.

"Yes, but first you must weed the garden."

Hee and her mother laughed as they left for the city.

Kwan's heart was heavy. The garden was filled with weeds.

She went outside and was surprised by a large brown cow who said, "I'll eat the weeds."

"Yes, please!" Kwan said.

The cow chomped all the weeds in a flash.

Suddenly, a flock of songbirds appeared in the sky, carrying a lovely robe and slippers. "For the strong one," they sang.

Thrilled, Kwan dashed down the road to the bridge crossing the river. She tripped and fell. One of her slippers splashed into the water. "Oh no!" cried Kwan, watching the slipper float away.

Kwan hobbled home and hid the gown and slipper in an old trunk.

Meanwhile, a young prince was traveling to the festival. Thirsty, he stopped by the river for a drink. He put his lips into the cold, rushing water, and a beautiful slipper floated by.

"Pretty slipper, pretty lady?" he asked as he grabbed the slipper.

"Pretty lady," sang the birds flying above.

"I must find her," he declared.

The prince traveled to many farms, asking every young woman to try on the slipper. Arriving at Kwan's farm, he showed it to Hee and Kwan.

Hee shoved Kwan to the side, saying, "It's mine!"

"You are not polite," said the prince. "Your sister will try first."

Kwan slipped her foot into the slipper.

"You are strong and beautiful," he said. "Please marry me."

Smiling, Kwan said, "Yes."

The songbirds swirled above. Happy was their song.

If the Shoe Fits
Two Cinderella Stories

Use details from *If the Shoe Fits: Two Cinderella Stories* to answer these questions with a partner.

1. **Make Connections** How are the two fairy tales alike? What are the most important differences between them?

2. Mrs. Fortuna consoles Zoey when she loses her shoe. Think about a time when you lost something. What made you feel better?

3. If Mrs. Fortuna and the songbirds had not been in the fairy tales, how else could the girls have solved their problems?

Talking Tip

Complete the sentence to add to what your partner says.

My idea is _____.

Write a Comparison

PROMPT Shoes are an important part of both stories. Compare Zoey's shoes with Kwan's shoes. How are their parts in the stories alike? How are they different?

PLAN First, make a list of details about Zoey's shoes. Then, make a list of details about Kwan's shoes. Look for details in the text and illustrations about how they look, where they come from, and what happens to them.

Zoey's shoes	Kwan's shoes

WRITE Now write sentences comparing Zoey's and Kwan's shoes. Use the details in your chart to explain how they are alike and different. Remember to:

- Describe how Zoey and Kwan feel about their shoes.

- Add an apostrophe to show ownership, like *Kwan's shoes*.

_____

_____

_____

_____

_____

_____

_____

_____

_____

Prepare to Read

GENRE STUDY **Fairy tales** are old stories that have made-up characters and events that could not happen.

MAKE A PREDICTION Preview "The Elves and the Shoemaker." A poor shoemaker needs help. How do you think he will get the help he needs?

_____

_____

_____

_____

_____

_____

_____

SET A PURPOSE Read to find out how the shoemaker gets the help he needs.

The Elves and the Shoemaker

READ What problem does the shoemaker have? <u>Underline</u> it.

Long ago, there was a kind shoemaker. He worked hard but did not make much money. One night, he went to bed feeling worried. He only had enough material to make one more pair of shoes. He would need to sell them for a good price.

The next morning, the shoemaker was amazed. In his workshop, he found the prettiest shoes he had ever seen! He sold them for a very good price. With the money, he bought material to make two more pairs of shoes.

The shoemaker felt grateful. He felt curious, too. Who was his mystery helper? ▶

Close Reading Tip
Number the main events on this page in order.

READ How is the shoemaker's problem solved?

Close Reading Tip

Write a **C** when you make a connection to an event in your life.

That night, he went to bed feeling happy. The next morning, he was amazed again! He found two beautiful pairs of shoes that he sold for a very, very good price.

This happened night after night. The shoemaker wanted to thank his helper. One night he stayed up late. To his surprise, three little barefoot elves entered his workshop and got right to work. The next night, the elves got a surprise. The shoemaker had made tiny pairs of boots just for them!

To thank the shoemaker, the elves showed him how to make fancy shoes. The shoemaker was never poor again.

CHECK MY UNDERSTANDING

Which events are repeated? How are those events an important part of the story?

_____

_____

_____

WRITE ABOUT IT Compare "The Elves and the Shoemaker" to the Cinderella stories. How is kindness an important part of each story? Use details about the characters to support your answer.

_____

_____

_____

_____

_____

_____

_____

_____

_____

_____

_____

Prepare to View

GENRE STUDY **Videos** are short movies that give you information or something for you to watch for enjoyment. As you watch *Those Clever Crows*, notice:

- how pictures, sounds, and words work together
- what the video is about
- information about the topic
- the tone or mood of the video

SET A PURPOSE Ask yourself what happens and why to make **cause and effect** connections about the video. A cause is something that makes something else happen. An effect is what happens because of the cause.

Build Background: Crows

THOSE CLEVER CROWS

from *The New York Times*

As You View Are crows clever? You decide! Watch the crows'
behavior. Think carefully about how the words help you
understand what the crows are doing. What do you think those
crows must be thinking?

Turn and Talk

THOSE CLEVER **CROWS**

from *The New York Times*

Use details from *Those Clever Crows* to answer these questions with a partner.

1. **Cause and Effect** What do the crows want to make happen? How do their actions help them reach their goal?

2. How are the crows in the video like the crows in the fable? How are they different?

3. Do you think *Those Clever Crows* is a good title for this video? Use details from the video to explain your ideas.

Talking Tip

Wait for your turn to speak. Talk about your feelings and ideas clearly.

I feel that _____.

Let's Wrap Up!

(?) Essential Question

What lessons can we learn from the characters in stories?

Pick one of these activities to show what you have learned about the topic.

1. Learn Your Lesson

Think of a lesson that kids can use in their everyday lives. Then write your own fable or fairy tale that teaches that lesson. Look back at the texts for ideas. See how many of those characters you can include in your new story!

2. Story Catalog

Make a catalog of things fables or fairy tales need. Look back at the texts for ideas. Then draw pictures of characters, settings, or objects you might find in those kinds of stories. Label each picture.

Word Challenge

Can you use the word moral in your catalog?

My Notes

Glossary

A

argue [är′gyo͞o]   When you argue, you speak in an angry way that shows you do not agree. Do not **argue** with your brother.

B

beamed [bēmd]   Someone who beamed gave a big smile. Caleb **beamed** when he read the funny story.

believe [bĭ-lēv′]   When you believe something, you think it is true. I **believe** that it will rain today.

bind [bīnd]   When you bind something, you tie it up. He will **bind** the books together with string.

blamed [blāmd]   When you are blamed, someone thinks you did something wrong. The kids **blamed** each other for the mess.

booming [bo͞om′ĭng]   Something that is booming is loud like thunder. The **booming** sounds let us know that the fireworks show had started.

C

chore [chôr]   A chore is a job you must do. His **chore** is to take out the trash.

clever [klĕv′ər]   Someone who is clever is very smart. My dog is **clever** and knows many tricks.

clue [klo͞o]   A clue is information that helps you find an answer. The open door was a **clue** that the lock needed to be fixed.

compromise [kŏm′prə-mīz′]   A compromise is when people agree to something by each giving up a little of what they want. The team agreed on a **compromise**.

cozy [kō′zē]   A place that is cozy is comfortable. The fireplace made the room very **cozy**.

D

dashed [dăsht]   If you dashed, you ran quickly. My dad **dashed** out the door to get to work on time.

decision [dĭ-sĭzh′ən]   When you make a decision, you make up your mind about something. I will make a **decision** about what to have for a snack.

disagreement [dĭs′ə-grē′mənt]   In a disagreement, people have different ideas about things. They had a **disagreement** about what game to play.

disturb [dĭ-stûrb′]   When you disturb someone, you bother that person. Please do not **disturb** me while I'm sleeping.

dragged [drăgd]   If you dragged something, you worked hard to pull it along the ground. The boy **dragged** the heavy suitcase across the floor.

E

excuses [ĭk-skyo͞os′ĭz]   Excuses are reasons why you cannot do something. He tried to make **excuses** for breaking the pitcher, but then he just apologized.

F

frown [froun]   A frown is a sad or angry look. The boy had a **frown** on his face.

fulfill [fo͝ol-fĭl′]   When you **fulfill** something, you make it happen. I always **fulfill** a promise.

G

greedy [grē′dē]   Someone who is greedy wants more than what is fair. Todd was being **greedy** with the popcorn.

H

hesitant [hĕz′ĭ-tənt]   If you are hesitant, you do something slowly because you are not sure about it. At first, Dan was **hesitant** to try the salad.

hobbled [hŏb′əld]   If you hobbled, you walked in a slow, uneven way. The boy **hobbled** home after he hurt his leg.

I

invited [ĭn-vīt′ĭd]   When you are invited to a party, you have been asked to come. My big brother **invited** me to go to the talent show with him and his friends.

J

jealous [jĕl′əs]   If you are jealous, you feel angry because you want what someone else has. I felt **jealous** when Emma won first place.

journey [jûr′nē]   A journey is a trip from one place to another. The map helped Cheri plan her **journey**.

M

moral [môr′əl, mŏr′əl]   A moral is a lesson in a story. The **moral** of the story is to keep trying.

mumbled [mŭm′bəld]   If you mumbled, you spoke quietly and not very clearly. She **mumbled** something that I did not understand.

musical [myōō′zĭ-kəl]   Something that is musical has a tune. A trumpet is a **musical** instrument.

N

narrow [năr′ō]   Something that is narrow is thin and has little space. It was hard for cars and bikes to fit together on the very **narrow** street.

nearby [nîr′bī′]   Someone who is nearby is close to where you are. My friend lives in a **nearby** house.

P

pause [pôz]   If you pause, you stop what you are doing for a short time. The speaker will **pause** so we can ask questions.

persuade [pər-swād′]   When you persuade, you try to get others to feel or think as you do. Please **persuade** her to join the fun.

plain [plān]   A plain is a flat piece of land with few trees. We saw beautiful flowers on the **plain**.

plead [plēd]   When you plead, you ask someone in a strong, hopeful way. We **plead** with our mother to let us go to the party.

pleasure [plĕzh′ər]   Pleasure is a feeling of happiness or joy. It is always a **pleasure** to see you.

practice [prăk′tĭs]   Practice is when you do something over and over to get better at it. I try to **practice** piano every day.

R

rattled [răt′ld]   Something that rattled made many short, shaking noises. The coins **rattled** in my pocket.

relate [rĭ-lāt′]   If you relate to someone, you know how the person feels. I can **relate** to how the character in this story is feeling.

respectful [rĭ-spĕkt′fəl]   Respectful words are words that are polite and kind. The players are **respectful** of each other.

S

scoots [sko͞ots]   When someone scoots, he or she moves very quickly. He **scoots** out the door so he won't miss the bus.

screams [skrēmz]   When someone screams, he or she yells loudly. She **screams** with excitement on her favorite ride in the amusement park.

scurries [skûr′ēz, skŭr′ēz] When someone scurries, he or she moves with short, fast steps. The chipmunk **scurries** across the yard.

sense [sĕns] Something that makes sense is easy to understand. It makes **sense** to practice before the big game.

shove [shŭv] When you shove something, you push it hard. Ian will **shove** the wagon for his sister.

skill [skĭl] If you have great skill at something, you do that thing really well. Ethel can bake with great **skill**, and she loves to share with her friends.

speech [spēch] A speech is a talk you give to an audience. My friend gave an inspiring **speech** after she won an award for her good citizenship.

steaming [stēm′ĭng] If something is steaming, it is very hot. The soup was **steaming**, so we had to wait a few minutes for it to cool.

superb [sŏŏ-pûrb′] Something that is superb is the very best. The celebration we had for my grandfather's birthday was **superb**!

T

tackled [tăk′əld] If you tackled someone, you pushed the person to the ground. He **tackled** the player with the football.

threatening [thrĕt′n-ĭng] People who are threatening to do something are warning they will do it. The group is **threatening** to quit if they don't get their own way.

thrilled [thrĭld] When you are thrilled, you are very excited. The kids were **thrilled** to go camping.

V

version [vûr′zhən]   A version is a different or changed form of something. We played a new **version** of the game.

W

wrinkled [rĭng′kəld]   You wrinkled up your face if you tightened muscles to make folds and lines in your skin. The baby **wrinkled** his little forehead.

Y

yanked [yăngkd]   If you **yanked** something, you pulled it hard and fast. The whole team **yanked** on the rope during the game of tug of war.

Index of Titles and Authors

"American Hero, An" 80

Be a Hero! Work It Out! 110

"Best Name, The" 36

"Best View, The" 184

Big Red Lollipop 14

Cooley, Ruben 110

Crow, a Lion, and a Mouse!
  Oh, My!, A 152

DeSpain, Pleasant 188

"Elves and the Shoemaker,
  The" 202

Fleming, Lisa 166

Gingerbread for Liberty! 58

Hollywood Chicken 166

"How to Find a Story" 148

How to Read a Story 126

Hubbard, Crystal 152

"I Respectfully Disagree!" 54

If the Shoe Fits: Two Cinderella
  Stories 188

Khan, Rukhsana 14

Lachtman, Ofelia Dumas 84

Messner, Kate 126

"More Than One Way to Win" 106

Nelson, Robin 40

Pepita and the Bully 84

Rockliff, Mara 58

Those Clever Crows 206

"Wind and the Sun, The" 162

Working with Others 40

Acknowledgments

Big Red Lollipop by Rukhsana Khan. Illustrated by Sophie Blackall. Text copyright © 2010 by Rukhsana Khan. Illustrations copyright © 2010 by Sophie Blackall. Reprinted by permission of Viking Children's Books, an imprint of Penguin Young Readers Group, a division of Penguin Random House LLC and Charlotte Sheedy Literary Agency.

Gingerbread for Liberty! (retitled from *Gingerbread for Liberty!: How a German Baker Helped Win the American Revolution*) by Mara Rockliff, illustrated by Vincent X. Kirsch. Text copyright © 2015 by Mara Rockliff. Illustrations copyright © 2015 by Vincent X. Kirsch. Reprinted by permission of Houghton Mifflin Harcourt Publishing Company and the Andrea Brown Literary Agency.

How to Read a Story by Kate Messner. Illustrated by Mark Siegel. Text copyright © 2015 by Kate Messner. Illustrations copyright © 2015 by Mark Siegel. Reprinted by permission of Chronicle Books LLC.

Pepita and the Bully/Pepita y la peleonera by Ofelia Dumas Lachtman, illustrated by Alex Pardo DeLange. Spanish translation by Gabriela Baeza Ventura. Text copyright © 2011 by Ofelia Dumas Lachtman. Illustrations copyright © 2011 by Alex Pardo DeLange. Reprinted by permission of Arte Público Press - University of Houston.

Excerpt from *Working with Others* by Robin Nelson. Text copyright © 2006 by Lerner Publishing Group, Inc. Reprinted with the permission of Lerner Publications Company, a division of Lerner Publishing Group, Inc.

Credits